A Look Inside the Modern Craft Movement

For those already in the Craft, and for those who stand outside the ritual circle wondering if it is the place for them, *Witchcraft Today, Book One: The Modern Craft Movement* brings together the writings of nine well-known Neopagans who give a cross-section of the beliefs and practices of this diverse and fascinating religion.

The contributors live in cities, small towns and rural areas, from California to Ireland, and they have all claimed a magical birthright—that lies open to any committed person—of healing, divination, counseling, and working with the world's cycles.

Written specifically for this volume, the articles examine the history of Witchcraft's revival, Pagan festivals, seasonal and magical rites, healing, sex magic, the roles of men and women in the Craft, ways to preserve the Earth, rituals for the solitary practitioner, guidelines for dealing with the law and media, shamanism, and Pagan life in a 9-to-5 world.

Also provided in this volume are additional resources for Wiccans and others interested in the Craft, including lists of publications, mail-order suppliers, Pagan organizations, computer bulletin boards, and special-interest resources.

As an extra feature, the "Principles of Wiccan Belief"—adopted in 1974 by a group of American Witches meeting in Minneapolis—are restated here in their entirety.

About the Editor
Chas S. Clifton holds a master's degree in religious studies with an emphasis on the development of new religious movements. He lives in the Upper Arkansas Valley of Colorado where he writes about Western esoteric traditions.

To Write to the Publisher
If you would like more information about this book, please write to the publisher in care of Llewellyn Worldwide. The publisher appreciates hearing from you and learning of your enjoyment of this book and how it has helped you. Llewellyn Worldwide cannot guarantee that every letter can be answered, but all will be reviewed. Please write to:

LLEWELLYN PUBLICATIONS
c/o Llewellyn Worldwide
P.O. Box 64383, Dept. L377-9,
St. Paul, MN 55164-0383, U.S.A.

Please enclose a self-addressed, stamped envelope for reply, or $1.00 to cover costs. If outside the U.S.A., enclose international postal reply coupon.

Free Catalog from Llewellyn
For more than 90 years Llewellyn has brought its readers knowledge in the fields of metaphysics and human potential. Learn about the newest books in spiritual guidance, natural healing, astrology, occult philosophy and more. To get your free copy of *Llewellyn's New Worlds of Mind and Spirit*, send your name and address to:

Llewellyn's New Worlds of Mind and Spirit
P.O. Box 64383, Dept.L377-9,
St. Paul, MN 55164-0383, U.S.A.

Witchcraft Today

BOOK ONE

The Modern Craft Movement

Edited by

Chas S. Clifton

1996
Llewellyn Publications
St. Paul, Minnesota 55164-0383, U.S.A.

FIRST EDITION, 1992
Fourth Printing, 1996

Cover photography by Malcolm Brenner
Cover design by Christopher Wells and Terry Buske

Library of Congress Cataloging-in-Publication Data

The modern craft movement / edited by Chas S. Clifton
      p.   cm. – (Witchcraft today ; bk. 1)
     Includes bibliographical references.
     ISBN 0-87542-377-9
     1. Witchcraft. Paganism. I. Clifton, Chas S. II. Series.
    BF1566.M654   1992
    133.4'3—dc20   92-918
                                       CIP

Llewellyn Publications
A Division of Llewellyn Worldwide , Ltd.
P.O. Box 64383, St. Paul, MN 55164-0383, U.S.A.

For Mary, a natural-born priestess,
and in memory of Charles R.F. Seymour,
who showed how to be both a historian and
a high priest of the Pagan Mysteries

Other Books in This Series

CONTENTS

Introduction

Witchcraft, the Magical Religion

Since the 1950s, when a small group of English Witches first went public about their religion, many books have been published to give insiders' views on the Pagan religion of Witchcraft (also called Wicca or just "the Craft"). At the same time, Witchcraft has no holy scriptures; no one may cite chapter and verse from any holy book to prove that his or her position on some issue is the right one. As a religion, Witchcraft turns the typical religious pyramid hierarchy upside-down; every Witch is at least theoretically a leader; there are no large congregations. Wicca has no pope or president; anyone claiming to be "queen (or king) of the Witches," "a member of the High Council of Twelve" or any such thing may be assumed to be a liar. But at the same time there are a multitude of national, regional and local organizations; these may have officers and budgets and may vote on items of business like any other nonprofit corporations. Particularly in the United States, some groups have taken the steps outlined by Pete Pathfinder in "Witchcraft and the

Law" and become legally recognized religious bodies, even participating in ecumenical councils. And no religious tradition more openly displays its "magical" or "supernatural" side, yet Witches are not hostile to science and do not fit the stereotype of the "fundamentalist" believer who attempts to ignore any information that does not fit into the universe described by his holy book. A Witch is never asked to shut off his or her brain in order to "have faith."

Perhaps then these paradoxes and such cheerful organizational anarchy are represented better by an anthology than by one person's writing. Only an anthology could begin to give a cross-section of the beliefs and practices of today's Neopagan Witchcraft. The contributors to this one have written from their own experiences; they have not simply copied the work of someone who came before. They have done all they could to make this book interesting both to people already in the Craft and to those who stand outside the ritual circle wondering if it is the place for them.

The contributors live in cities, small towns and rural areas, from California to Ireland, but they have one thing in common: they have claimed a magical birthright of healing, divination, counseling and working with the world's cycles that lie open to any committed person—without the need to get permission from some holy highup leader. No wonder Witchcraft baffles and enrages those so-called religious authorities who crave the power to tell their followers how to live. Modern Witchcraft may only be a few decades old, but its message is ancient. As Witches we respect ability and knowledge, but we do not permit anyone to stand between us and the spiritual realm. And much to the confusion of the few sociologists and anthropologists who have tried to deal with modern Witchcraft, we are not simply escapists from the modern world. I have known Witches to be electrical engineers, police officers, librarians, journalists, artists, schoolteachers, businesspeople, farmers, computer systems analysts, college professors, nurses, diesel mechanics, members of the Armed Forces, and on and on. Despite their different backgrounds and upbringings, most will say that when they found the Craft, they "came home." They share a certain stubborn vision and a certain courage.

Today's Witches have found a spiritual path which integrates all the concerns of their lives instead of saying that some things were "holy" and other things were "profane." No Witch, for example, would ever say that it is necessary to avoid sexual relationships in order to be "more spiritual." Instead, we say that sexuality is one way to unite with divine forces; the chapter entitled "Sex Magic" gives some suggestions on how this is done.

By its existence, Witchcraft criticizes the idea of religious evolution, the notion that "primitive" people began as animists worshiping the spirits of trees, pools or animals, then "progressed" to a more refined system of many gods and thence to monotheism, the worship of one god. To the Witch, all three outlooks can be handled simultaneously; the world is a shimmering fabric of divine forces that may be called upon and that may indeed proceed from One Source, but that One Source is beyond intellectual description. Idolizing Progress, people too often forget the truths that the so-called primitive people knew—whether they were the truths of keeping population in balance with resources or the insights of dealing with unseen forces. (Once the primitives may have offered human sacrifices, but we modern people no longer do that; we merely suffer "inevitable social consequences of economic changes" and let the victims live in cardboard boxes.)

Witches do not so much "worship Nature" as we

reject any so-called spiritual teaching that splits us from Nature, or that would suggest that the Earth, its processes and its inhabitants do not reflect and participate in the multitude of seen and unseen realities. We do not hold ourselves apart as superior to Nature, but we know we will always return to her and through her. The Pagan attitude is contrary to the ancient gnostic teaching (which always sneaks into the monotheistic religions) that our souls are "imprisoned" in our bodies. The reality is more complex; in brief, we could say that the spirit influences the body and the body influences the spirit. Most Witches follow some form of reincarnational teaching which offers the comfort that even if one body becomes completely useless, another one can be taken as the spirit moves on.

A short note about terminology. "Witch" is a word frequently tossed around to mean everything from an angry, outspoken woman to a worshiper of the Christian Devil, a being whose existence Pagan Witches consider to have been unduly emphasized (if not outright invented) by Christians as a means of passing on the blame for all the evil that humans do. Some writers have tried to trace the word "witch" back to roots meaning "to know" (as in "wit") or "to bend (reality)." But when the search is carried back to Proto-Indo-European—the ancient hypothetical ancestor of a large language family that includes everything from Sanskrit to Latin to English—the root of "witch" is "weik-" a root of words connected with magic and religious notions. In other words, witch means witch.

Old English, the form of our language spoken from the Anglo-Saxon invasions of the 5th century until the early Middle Ages, roughly 800 years, had grammatical gender like Spanish or German. Consequently, there were separate words for masculine-witch and feminine-witch. These were "wicca" (pronounced "witch-ah" or "weech-ah") and "wicce" (pronounced "witch-eh" or "weech-ay"). As English changed, becoming simpler, the unstressed second syllable disappeared, leaving "witch," which was masculine or feminine as appropriate.

The term "Wicca," now pronounced with hard c's, was brought back in the 1940s and 1950s, however, by English Witches such as Gerald Gardner who wanted a new term to describe their revived form of Pagan religion. By using the word Wicca they hoped to avoid the tired old image of the witch as a worshiper of the Christian Devil. Likewise, in this book Wicca is used by some contributors interchangeably with Witchcraft, and Wiccan interchanges with Witch (capitalized) to mean a follower of the modern Pagan magical religion as opposed to any other meaning that may be attached to the word "witch."

Calling oneself a Witch, however, is more than a statement about participating in a polytheistic religion whose god and goddess, in their various manifestations, are honored and invoked through a yearly cycle as described in "Seasonal Rites / Magical Rites." That can be handled under the larger, more general term Pagan. If a Witch is a doer, a healer, a diviner, a traveler into unseen realms, he or she must be able to bring back something. For that reason, this book includes chapters on healing ("Witchcraft and Healing") and on Witchcraft's relationship with the broader idea of shamanism (see "Bone Beaters: Witchcraft and Shamanism"). Janet Farrar, co-author of the chapter on men's and women's roles in the Craft ("Men and Women in Witchcraft"), summarized the situation neatly when I first met her in 1978. At first people may be startled or skeptical when they learn you are a Witch, she said. Then, sooner or later, they bring you their problems. And, she added bluntly, "If they come to you with piles, you had better know where the 'hemorrhoid wort' grows!" (While I do not believe there is an herb called "hemorrhoid wort," a competent herbalist could ease the condition, and Janet's advice was worthwhile.) Valerie Voigt reports some similar experiences in "Being a Pagan in a 9-to-5 World," her account of blending Witchcraft with typical experiences as a working woman and mother.

To be real, Witchcraft must be more than a belief statement. It requires work on the "inner planes" and in the outer world. The Craft is not all sweetness and Light, but it also acknowledges and works with the necessities of death, Darkness and renewal. It is about dirt and flowers, blood and running water, sex and sickness, spells and household tools, old people teaching young people, intuition and spontaneity and simply "feeling the power." Witches always know that the power is raised to be used.

Magic and the Ritual Circle

Indoors or outdoors, Witches create a sacred area for religious celebration and magical working each time they gather. This area, referred to simply as "the circle," is actually a symbolic picture of the cosmos. Just as a stage set made up of a few flimsy walls and some pieces of furniture can effectively represent the interior of a house or a street scene, so the Witches' circle represents for a short time the forces that power the universe and provides a symbolic "stage" on which they may appear. Some covens may have permanent ritual areas, such as a place in a forest marked out by a circle of large stones, but even then the circle must be cast afresh each time. It is created not so much by having the right objects properly arranged, but through the concentration and imagination of the coveners themselves.

Some Witches used to contrast their approach to that

of the ceremonial magicians by saying that "the magicians cast a circle to keep dangers out; we cast a circle to keep the power in." This is understandable when we accept that the circle is a sort of psychic force field created by the people in it; for a time it glows to the inner sight (some Witches think of it as a sphere or egg more than a circle), permitting easier access to the Otherworld, but ultimately it is "shut off." (A correctly completed ritual should leave either a neutral psychic atmosphere or at most a sort of "bright" feeling; all energies summoned should have been equally dismissed.) The Witches' circle is the answer to the old question, "Where is the center of the Universe?" The response, of course, is "The center of the circle"—in other words, right where you are. The indwelling energies of some sites may make ritual easier there, perhaps because of a long history of powerful workings and expectations associated with them, but a circle may be cast anywhere.

We probably will never see Pagan temples surrounded by acres of asphalt-covered parking lots; for one thing, Witchcraft cringes at the idea of eradicating that much of the natural world in the name of Organized Religion. For another, Witchcraft as usually practiced is for small groups. A coven is like a basketball team: if one player on the court is just standing there studying his fingernails, his absence from play will be obvious. Likewise, when everyone is in the state of heightened psychic sensitivity that should result in ritual, someone's failure to contribute his or her energy to the circle will be obvious as a sort of "dead spot." (See "Witchcraft and Healing" for an example of this happening during a healing ritual.)

Within most covens, the circle is subdivided into four quarters named after the four psychological elements: Fire, Earth, Air and Water. They are capitalized because they are metaphors, categories in which to sort experiences, emotions or needs, clusters of psychological traits. It would be wrong, however, to say that Air, for example, is "only a metaphor." Is communication, the flow of information, mental activity, organizing and structuring of thought, only a metaphor? Of course not, but we designate all of that magically as taking place within the Realm of Air.

Witches come to the circle dressed in one of three ways, each way saying something about their attitudes toward what they are doing. One traditional way of celebrating and working within the circle is "skyclad" or nude. Gerald Gardner, co-founder of an important portion of modern Witchcraft (see "A Quick History of Witchcraft's Revival"), advocated ritual nudity. Gardner was also attracted to the "nudist" or "naturist" lifestyle outside of Witchcraft. Perhaps during his years as a British civil servant in some of the Asian colonies such as Malaya where the local people habitually wore fewer clothing than did visiting Englishmen, he came to the conclusion that if weather permitted clothing to be dispensed with, then there was no reason not to take it off. Nevertheless, the thought of naked men and women gathered together by candlelight in privacy continues to titillate a lot of people who are just convinced that Wiccan ritual is simply an excuse for a sexual orgy. To which many Witches will reply, if you want to have an orgy, have an orgy and don't bother to disguise it as religion. If it is any consolation, the same tired accusation of someone's religion being just an excuse for promiscuous sex has been used many times before. Some ancient Romans used it against followers of "exotic Oriental cults," including Christianity—those "love feasts" sounded suspicious. Christians in turn accused various heretics of the Middle Ages and the so-called witches of the later Middle Ages and Renaissance of meeting only for that purpose.

And so it goes.

To always equate nudity with sex is to miss some other points, however. Anyone who has attended skyclad workings knows that ritual nudity serves other purposes. One which was probably more important in the past than now is that it helps erase social differences. It is an equalizer. The person who came to the circle in an expensive designer dress and the person who came in a T-shirt and jeans are now, in the eyes of the gods, the same. More subtle than that, however, is that nudity is related to the fear of death. Witches, as mentioned, generally espouse some form of the doctrine of reincarnation. We believe that we are our bodies but we are also more than our bodies. To see our own and other people's nude bodies without the camouflage effect of clothing is to be reminded that they are not permanent. They grow, they age, they are changed by childbearing and other factors. Ultimately they must be left behind. Since so much of our cultural baggage is devoted to denying that fact, it is not surprising that Witchcraft, one of the most pragmatic of religions, brings it out into the open.

Last of all, nudity contributes to the theatrical side of ritual because for most people it is a non-ordinary experience—unless they live in very hot climates, perhaps. We do not customarily interact with groups of other people while naked. To do so sends a message to our Unconscious (called in some traditions the Child Self or the Younger Self): "This is different. This is special. Let the magic happen." Ultimately it is the Child Self that holds the key to the Otherworld, but one of the secrets of magic is that the Child Self does not respond well to "reason" and to argument. It responds better to emotion, pictures and situations; it can be called out to play, but it rarely can be lectured.

Some covens mark their rituals as "special" through

wearing special clothing, usually long robes. Now in some parts of the world such as parts of North Africa, a long, loose robe with a pointed hood is standard male attire, but ever since the gradual swing away from long robes and toward divided lower garments (handier for horseback riding in cold weather) in Europe in the late Middle Ages, long robes for men have been associated with only certain groups, primarily Catholic monks and priests and also university professors—who themselves at one time were also all in holy orders. The robe, therefore, masks social differences, is warmer than going naked, and in a culture where it is not everyday attire, seems special, perhaps "holy," and thus appropriate for wear during the Witchcraft ritual, "the time that is not a time in the place that is not a place." And since modern women generally do not wear floor-length dresses every day, when a woman dons a ritual robe, she too can easily feel that she is preparing for a non-ordinary event.

Some people, however, may not wish to meet skyclad (if only for reasons of physical comfort), and may have reasons for not wearing robes. Their alternative is to wear street clothes. This might even be required by the ritual itself. For instance, one Colorado coven used to carry out a winter solstice ritual that required participants to leave the indoor ritual space (a rented theater) at one point and, one by one, walk a circuit of several public mineral springs within the central part of their small town. At each of the springs someone would be waiting to carry out part of the ceremony. This ceremony had to be carried out on a cold December night and in public, with traffic on the streets, yet the participants had to remain in "sacred space" at the same time and not attract attention. Under the circumstances, non-ordinary clothing would not have been a practical choice. On the other hand, to react against wearing robes or other special clothing just because it seems affected is to take a magical risk. It hampers the necessary theatrical aspect of successful ritual working, just as if a troupe of actors said, "We're going to put on a play but we won't wear any costumes to indicate our characters." To meet, celebrate and work magic in our street clothes is not impossible, but it means that our Younger Selves have to get the message to come out and play through other means than sight: music, pure imagination, scent, movement, and so forth.

The Witches' circle symbolically bridges the gap between the mundane world—the world of history, jobs, school, and all our physical and mental concerns—and the Otherworld. The term Otherworld takes in whatever realms our spirits may visit before birth and after death—and at times in dreams. It is the "astral plane" of many occultists, the "happy hunting ground" of Native American tribes, Paradise, the realm of ideas and pure forms that underlie our attempts to make these ideas manifest in our material world. (When we die, some Witches say, we are born into the Otherworld; when we die in the Otherworld, likewise, we are born into Middle Earth, the material world.) Through the circle we attune ourselves to those divine forces called the gods and personified in countless ways by different cultures.

Modern Witches are fond of a saying employed by the English occultist Dion Fortune: "All gods are one god, and all goddesses are one goddess, and there is one initiator." Another paradox, however, is that the gods are most successfully invoked by name. It is something like listening to the radio: one does not just turn on the FM band in general, but tunes in a specific station. And when one is listening to one station, all the other stations do not cease to exist. The gods, in the Pagan view, do not require our worship because they are so wonderful for creating the world and we are such miserable sinners grateful to be spared from destruction for our intolerable wickedness. However this world, Middle Earth, was created, we may never know all its purposes; to look at it as a school is as useful an approach as any. It is certainly better for all its inhabitants if we look at the Earth as "the body of the Goddess" than if we see it as a disposable Creation that we cannot wait to get out of, discarding it like a used tissue.

Photo by Chas S. Clifton

Within the circle, meanwhile, the Witches' Goddess and God are present symbolically through objects and at times through certain participants. The Goddess, mother of physical creation, source of inspiration, receiver of the dead, is usually symbolized by a cup or chalice. She is not abstractly "believed in"; she is experienced and felt. Likewise her male counterpart (to the extent that the spiritual principles animating the universe can be said to have gender) is symbolized by a knife called the *athame* (pronounced as three syllables with the accent usually on the first). Athame is a word of mysterious origin although some people believe it comes from a Greek term meaning "deathless." In the material world, the principle of action is symbolized as male while matter is symbolized as passive and female; in the Otherworld, it only follows that the principles are reversed. (See "Men and Women in Witchcraft" for more on these teachings.) Since the circle is seen as an opening to the Otherworld, a male Witch may hold the cup and a female the athame as they are brought together in a symbolic sexual act that shows the union of the two divine powers and the transmission of the Witches' purpose between the two realms.

That purpose is what gives our magical religion its special quality. "Magic," of course, is a loaded word, slippery to define and frequently negative in connotation. To Witches, who are practical people, all religions have their magical sides, but some will not admit it. Anytime that people attempt to influence the outcome of events rather than simply putting themselves in tune with them, they are "working magic." They may call it praying, for example, but it is magic all the same. Frequently outside observers miss this point; they confuse "spells" or "magical phrases" with magic. Sociologists of religion and other scholars have spilled a lot of ink trying to enforce a distinction between a "priest" who has a congregation and a "magician" who has a clientele. In real life, however, the roles always become blurred. To "pray for peace" or "to seek salvation" are magical acts insofar as they seek to change present conditions.

What approach, then, does the Craft take? First, it sets out a simple ethical guideline, sometimes referred to as the Law of Threefold Return. "Whatever you do returns to you threefold." Or, as an old slang expression puts it, "What goes around, comes around." This is another version of the Golden Rule ("Do unto others as you would have them do unto you"); it recognizes also that it is impossible to find peace while smoldering with inner violence or to make money while being obsessed with one's own poverty.

When Witches prepare a ritual, then, we have—on the surface—two choices. We can make it purely a ritual of celebration or attunement, or we can say we are gathering to "raise power" for a particular purpose such as helping someone to find a new job or to overcome a sickness. The first may seem more "priestly"; as Pauline Campanelli writes in "Seasonal Rites / Magical Rites," we are attuning ourselves to the creative force of the Cosmos. But what for? That force or power has to be used for something; it has to be taken into our lives that we may keep going on day after day, and sometimes certain situations may require an extra helping of it. That brings us to the second choice, the working with a purpose. At the same time, by attuning ourselves to the Cosmos we may learn that at times it is useless to oppose the way things are going; for this reason, many seasoned magical workers perform some type of divination in advance of any working to see whether it is worth the effort.

When we enter the ritual circle, then, we are actually operating on several levels at once. Here it is helpful to return to the three-stage model of the self that many Witches use. The Unconscious (or subconscious) Self, as mentioned above, is sometimes referred to as the Lower Self, Child Self or Younger Self; the last two terms help us picture its mixture of creativity, playfulness and undisciplined random qualities. It also has the important job of controlling the physical body. Whereas the Middle Self (see below) sleeps, the Child Self never sleeps.

The self that is reading these words is the Ego or the Talking Self or Middle Self. Some Asian traditions refer to it as the "monkey mind," full of chatter. It is the thinker and manager that gets things done on Middle Earth: it goes to school, goes to work, and balances the checkbook, but deprived of spiritual guidance can worry itself into complete paralysis. It is a mistake, however, to say that it is "not spiritual" and hence must be controlled or even abandoned. The secret is learning when to ignore it. For example, a person who works magically for a better job has to ignore the Middle Self's chatter about "You'll never make it. You're stuck here forever." But when the opportunity comes, the Middle Self has to do the work in an intelligent way, or the whole working was in vain.

More remote from the Middle Self is the Higher Self, or Superconscious (some people equate it with the "guardian angel"). This is the truly un-sensed part of us, the part that cannot normally be reached through reasoning. Magic, however, tells us that the way to the Upper is through the Lower. One way that "reason" of a kind can help us understand the High Self's purposes is through the interpretation of dreams, which themselves are the Child Self's stories about what is going on. The Lower Self also communicates the Higher Self's messages through "coincidences" and body changes. But it is the High Self that truly opens into the Cosmos, that receives the divine energies. In order to do this, it needs the energy fed to it by the Middle Self and particularly the Lower Self. Ritual raises this energy.

In ritual we raise this energy partly by getting the Lower or Child Self's attention. The effect of costuming— or its lack—has been mentioned. Scent (as from incense), sound, vision, physical movement (such as dancing or breathing techniques), and, finally, imagination all contribute to raising energy so that it can be passed to the

High Self and on for its purpose. The energy of a healing, for example, would be received by the High Self of the sick person and then his or her Child Self, which controls the body.

It is the Low or Younger Self's "childish" nature that produces the very real phenomenon of "beginner's luck" in magic. This frequently is misread by the Middle Self in one of two ways. The Middle Self either thinks, "Wow, I'm a great magician! Look what I did!" or—and I have seen both reactions happen—it is so shocked by success that it did not really expect that the person runs screaming into the arms of a nice authoritarian religion like some form of fundamentalist Protestantism that will provide all the answers from then on and require no further thought on the believer's part. This latter reaction explains countless stories about the "two 15 year olds and the Ouija board," how after getting some "answers" they suddenly decide that the whole thing is scary and demonic and vow never to touch it again. They failed to understand that the Child Self enjoyed the new game for a while, but failing to feel appreciated, got bored. Meanwhile the Middle Self, which should have used its powers of reason, moderation and common sense to evaluate what was received, instead spun a web of fantasy.

A Word to Newcomers

Before I found the Craft, I dreamt of it—literally. Without going into great detail, it is enough to say that the dream's feeling was like standing in a dark forest looking at group of happy strangers around a campfire and hoping to be invited to come sit down with them.

Finding a coven, let alone the "right" coven, is not always easy. You, the newcomer, may feel that you are too old, too young, too geographically isolated, too poor, over-educated, not educated enough, too "normal," too "different," not "psychic" enough or cut off in some other way from what you think is going on. None of these mainly self-imposed barriers is necessarily a final one, but each can be real enough at the time. Meanwhile, however, there are steps you can take in both the mundane world and the world of magic.

As is described more fully in "A Quick History of Witchcraft's Revival," Witchcraft's renaissance in the 1950s in Britain and the 1960s in North America was often accompanied by the idea that a person had to be born into the right family or formally initiated before he or she could begin to do anything. By the late 1970s this idea had begun to disappear, replaced with the concept that self-initiation was valid. We have to remember that an "initiation" is not something like a diploma or a college degree showing that the recipient has *completed* something so much as it is a formal announcement in several different realities that she or he is *beginning* something. The word comes from the same Latin root as "initial," as in "her initial effort." A magical initiation may signify that the initiate has completed certain study or work and is therefore "qualified" to do certain things, but it also means that the initiate is starting on a long, long journey.

If you are such a seeker, you can structure your own initial "course of study." Heather O'Dell's "The Solo Witch," is for you in particular. Read, study, meditate, and do not feel ashamed that your ritual work begins solo. Many others have done the same and most of them have learned the same magical lesson, that you attract what you think about and work toward. Sooner or later they made the contacts they were seeking.

The resource chapter at the end of this book will help you with one kind of contacts. The Pagan press is far-reaching and ever-changing, but one of its major functions has been to put people in touch with each other. In addition, now there are Pagan electronic bulletin boards too; some may shut down, but others will arise, and the printed newsletters can help you to locate their electronic counterparts. In addition, these newsletters and magazines will carry ads for bookstores and other shops that are meeting places. (These exist primarily in large cities.) You may walk in and see an announcement for a Pagan study group that is set up to introduce people to the Craft and guide them to a group where they will feel at home. Regional and National Pagan festivals (described by Oz in "An Insider's Look at Pagan Festivals") have a similar effect; attending a successful festival is like being suddenly put into psychic overdrive and being made aware of potentials and possibilities you never knew of before.

One of your first magical intentions may be to locate compatible souls. For example, Janet and Stewart Farrar, in "Men and Women in Witchcraft," describe how they used simple sex magic to create the nucleus of a new coven after they had moved from England to Ireland. Of course, when the opportunity or "coincidence" that they had magically created occurred, they were ready to make use of it in the here-and-now; doing magic requires balanced effort.

No one becomes a Witch overnight; that is why some covens traditionally wait a year and a day to initiate a newcomer. It makes sense to expose the seeker to the "wheel of the year" (see "Seasonal Rites / Magical Rites") first and to let him or her feel the rhythms of the unseen realms for at least that long. But even if you, a seeker, cannot find teachers in the flesh immediately, if your heart is pulling you toward the Craft, there is no need to wait to begin.

—Chas S. Clifton

PRINCIPLES OF WICCAN BELIEF

In 1974 one group of American Witches meeting in Minneapolis adopted the following group of principles. These principles are not required of anyone, but they do reflect the thinking of many modern Pagan Witches whether in the United States or elsewhere. The Council of American Witches finds it necessary to define modern Witchcraft in terms of the American experience and needs.

We are not bound by traditions from other times and other cultures, and owe no allegiance to any person or power greater than the Divinity manifest through our own being.

As American Witches we welcome and respect all teachings and traditions and seek to learn from all and to contribute our learning to all who may seek it.

It is in this spirit of welcome and cooperation that we adopt these few principles of Wiccan belief. In seeking to be inclusive, we do not wish to open ourselves to the destruction of our group by those on self-serving power trips, or to philosophies and practices contradictory to those principles. In seeking to exclude those whose ways are contradictory to ours, we do not want to deny participation with us to any who are sincerely interested in our knowledge and beliefs.

We therefore ask only that those who seek to identify with us accept those few basic principles.

1. We practice rites to attune ourselves with the natural rhythm of life forces marked by the full of the Moon and seasonal quarters and cross-quarters.

2. We recognize that our intelligence gives us a unique responsibility toward our environment. We seek to live in harmony with Nature, in ecological balance offering fulfillment to life and consciousness within an evolutionary concept.

3. We believe in a depth of power far greater than that apparent to the average person. Because it is far greater than ordinary, it is sometimes called "supernatural," but we see it as lying within that which is naturally potential to all.

4. We conceive of the Creative Power in the Universe as manifesting through polarity—as masculine and feminine—and that this same Creative Power lives in all people, and functions through the masculine and feminine. We value neither above the other.

5. We value sex as pleasure, as the symbol and embodi-

ment of life, and as the interaction source of energies used in magical practice and religious worship.

6. We recognize both an outer world and an inner, or psychological world—sometimes known as the Spiritual World, the Collective Unconscious, Inner Planes, etc.—and we see in the interaction of these two dimensions the basis for paranormal phenomena and magical exercises. We neglect neither dimension for the other, seeing both as necessary for our fulfillment.

7. We do not recognize any authoritarian hierarchy, but do honor those who teach, respect those who share their greater knowledge and wisdom, and acknowledge those who courageously give of themselves in leadership.

8. We see religion, magic, and wisdom in living as being united in the way one views the world and lives within it—a world view and philosophy of life which we identify as Witchcraft, the Wiccan Way.

9. Calling oneself "Witch" does not make a Witch—but neither does heredity itself nor the collecting of titles, degrees, and initiations. A Witch seeks to control the forces within her/himself that make life possible in order to live wisely and well without harm to others and in harmony with Nature.

10. We believe in the affirmation and fulfillment of life in a continuation of evolution and development of consciousness giving meaning to the Universe we know and our personal role within it.

11. Our only animosity towards Christianity, or towards any other religion or philosophy of life, is to the extent that its institutions have claimed to be "the only way" and have sought to deny freedom to others and to suppress other ways of religious practice and belief.

12. As American Witches we are not threatened by debates on the history of the Craft, the origins of various terms, the legitimacy of various aspects of different traditions. We are concerned with our present and our future.

13. We do not accept the concept of absolute evil nor do we worship any entity known as "Satan" or "the Devil" as defined by the Christian tradition. We do not seek power through the suffering of others nor accept that personal benefit can be derived only by denial to another.

14. We believe that we should seek within Nature that which is contributory to our health and well-being.

A Quick History of Witchcraft's Revival

by Chas S. Clifton

The Pagan religion of Witchcraft was reborn in the mid 20th century through the combined efforts of occultists, poets, folklorists and those important but little-known people who preserved parts of older Witch traditions. For some of these, recovering the traditions of Witchcraft was part of a larger effort to save old ways and lore in the face of growing industrial civilization. For others, it was a matter of inner inspiration, something that needed to be done because the clock of the cosmos or the voices of the Old Gods said it was time for it to be done. Others stumbled into their Pagan past when researching matters that on the surface seemed unrelated. All the people discussed here wrote books, and some of the most important books are listed at the end of this chapter. That is not to say that others did not contribute to the rebirth of Witchcraft as well, but the discussion that follows is tied to the books listed so that readers who wish to may follow up in greater detail.

Among the first people to discover the Old Religion in modern times was an American journalist, Charles Godfrey Leland (1824-1903). Leland, who traveled extensively from his hometown of Philadelphia, was fascinated by subcultures and people who resisted or who seemed about to be overwhelmed by "progress." He spent time with Native American medicine people and African-American voodooists, traveled with English Gypsies and learned their Romany language, and always sought out fortunetellers, herb doctors, and magical workers of all kinds. Besides many newspaper and magazine articles, he wrote a two-volume autobiography, a book on whether Chinese Buddhist monks might have sailed to the West Coast of America and a book on developing "the mystic will." In addition, he wrote works on Algonquin Indian legends, Gypsies and the Romany language, edited collections of folk songs and folk tales and co-edited a dictionary of "slang, jargon and cant." Leland was best known in his own time for a collection of comic poems in German-American dialect, *Hans Breitmann's Ballads*; today, however, his fame rests on a short book called *Aradia, or the Gospel of the Witches*.

In the 1880s Leland visited the region of Tuscany in northern Italy and met a woman called Maddalena, whom he identified as a *strega* or sorceress. "I employed her specially to collect among her sisters of the hidden spell in many places all the traditions of the olden time known to them," he wrote. In 1886 he heard of a manuscript that held all the doctrines of Italian Witchcraft and he urged Maddalena to find it, but it was not until 1897 that she delivered a copy in her own handwriting. His health failing, Leland rushed it into print after translating it into English and adding commentary; *Aradia* was published in London in 1899. Leland realized he had found something that was more than "folklore." He was struck by how the "witches' gospel" described the goddess Diana as creating the world, how parts of it resembled the ancient Pagan Roman religion, and by the work's anti-establishment overtones. *Aradia* (perhaps a dialect version of "Herodias," another old goddess name) was described as Diana's daughter. In the story Maddelena related, Diana was the Moon goddess, the fertile principle of cosmic darkness. Lucifer (from the Latin word for "light") was her brother the Sun god. Together they produced Aradia, who brought knowledge of magic to humankind to help people to live better and to overcome their oppressors, whether cruel landlords or fanatical churchmen.

Besides the creation story, *Aradia* contains many spells and magical formulas, instructions for preparing the ritual meal of the Italian Witches and a group of Italian folk tales in which the goddess Diana (or "Tana" in the local dialect) appears.

While Maddalena had written down much that her "sisters" transmitted orally, Leland was sure that a written book in the Latin language underlay her material, perhaps dating from the Renaissance when many scholars turned to recovering pre-Christian esoteric teaching. He rejoiced in what he had found, for he was certain that the tradition Maddalena represented was disappearing rapidly: "it is going—going—it is all but gone," he wrote.

About twenty years later, the idea that a Pagan "old religion" might have survived into Medieval (if not more recent) Britain was first set forth in the 1920s by a British archaeologist, Margaret Murray (1863-1963) of University College, London. She had worked mainly in Egypt until World War I interrupted her and her colleagues' efforts. Back in England she became ill and decided to convalesce in Glastonbury, a town associated with the legend of the Holy Grail:

> One cannot stay in Glastonbury without becoming interested in Joseph of Arimathea and the Holy Grail. As soon as I got back to London I did a careful piece of research, which resulted in a paper on Egyptian Elements in the Grail Romance .... Someone, I forget who, had once told me that the Witches obviously had a special form of religion, "for they danced around a black goat." As ancient religion is my pet subject this seemed to be in my line and during all the rest of the war I worked on Witches .... I had started with the usual idea that the Witches were all old women suffering from illusions about the Devil and that their persecutors were wickedly prejudiced and perjured. I worked only from contemporary records, and when I suddenly realized that the so-called Devil was simply a disguised man I was startled, almost alarmed, by the way the recorded facts fell into place and showed that the Witches were members of an old and primitive form of religion, and the records had been made by members of a new and persecuting form.

Murray produced three books based on this revelation. Unlike Leland, she did not use Italian sources but relied chiefly on witchcraft trial records of the late Middle Ages and Renaissance in England, Scotland, France and Germany. Her work was roundly criticized by folklorists and historians, but the idea that some sort of fertility cult had survived Christianity has been echoed by scholars studying such varied regions as Rumania and Italy. Murray detected primarily the worship of a male god, often represented with spreading stag's horns and known as Herne or Cernunnos (from the Latin for "The Horned One"). His image dates back centuries and was even carved in the stone ornamentation of medieval churches.

Two books published in the 1940s dealt with the Great Goddess and influenced the Witchcraft revival. *The*

White Goddess, by the English novelist and poet Robert Graves (1895-1986), argued that "the language of poetic myth anciently current in the Mediterranean and Northern Europe was a magical language bound up with popular religious ceremonies in honour of the Moon-goddess, or Muse, and that this remains the language of true poetry." Graves believed that medieval witches continued the worship of this goddess. Likewise, Gertrude Rachel Levy made a similar argument, working more from the viewpoint of art history rather than poetry, in *The Gate of Horn*.

Graves, at least, was solicited by certain modern Witches to take a more active role. He said he always refused. But another group of people—active occultists—began openly seeking the Western Way in the 1930s. Primary among them was Dion Fortune (1890-1946), who after being a member of the important early 20th-century British magical organization, the Order of the Golden Dawn, started her own, called the Society of Inner Light. She wrote a number of books on magic and mysticism, but it was her novels in particular, books such as *The Sea Priestess*, *Moon Magic*, *The Winged Bull* and *The Goat-Foot God*, that made her case for an enlightened return to the old Pagan ways with a balance of male and female divinity. Fortune and her associates such as Col. Charles Seymour and Christine Hartley believed that through ritual magic they could open a way for the Goddess to return to the modern world (this is the chief theme of *The Sea Priestess*). They also believed that persons drawn to magic in this life had usually been associated with esoteric schools in earlier lives, and that it was possible to find one's old companions and teachers again, whether they were currently incarnated or not.

Seymour (1880-1943), in particular, has not been duly recognized, for he stood somewhat in Fortune's

Dion Fortune

shadow. She headed the Society of the Inner Light; he was
her priest (as was also her husband, Dr. Thomas "Merl"
Evans) and an instructor of the school's students.
Seymour was a type that turns up occasionally in magical
groups, a military officer with a high degree of esoteric
wisdom. As an Army officer he served throughout the
British Empire; in 1930 he retired and became, in essence,
a Pagan theologian. His knowledge of Greek philosophy,
the ancient Mediterranean mystery religions, of early

Dr. Thomas "Merl" Evans

Christianity and of ancient history were matched by his personal experience with magic, a combination that is all too rare. He was the model for Colonel Brangwyn in Fortune's *The Winged Bull* and of the Priest of the Moon in *The Sea Priestess*. From a magical standpoint, Seymour and another of his magical partners, Christine Hartley, both made the link with the Old Gods that was further manifested by Gerald Gardner and other British Witches a few years later. Both Seymour and Hartley (who wrote *The Western Mystery Tradition*) were aware of Leland's *Aradia* and they believed they had at times made psychic contact with the Witch Cult of previous centuries although that was not their major area of concern.

Dion Fortune's Society of the Inner Light, while influential, was not the only group offering the hidden teachings of the Western Way in England of the 1930s. Gerald Gardner (1884-1964), a retired civil servant and avocational anthropologist with a long-time interest in magical religion, found another one after he retired from his work in Britain's Asian colonies and returned home to England. In the late 1930s he encountered a small group in Hampshire, in an area called the New Forest, whose members said they were carrying on the ancient Pagan religion of Witchcraft or Wicca. He was initiated in 1939, and later told a biographer that only when he heard the word Wicca did he know that "that which I had thought burnt out hundreds of years ago still survived." Like Charles Leland, he was excited as a folklorist to find the

Gerald B. Gardner

Old Religion, but unlike Leland he was initiated and totally committed himself to reviving and publicizing the Craft, the religion of the Great Goddess.

Gardner's return to England after a life spent mainly in Southeast Asia and his subsequent investigation of various esoteric groups coincided with the heyday of Dion Fortune's Society of the Inner Light. The possibility that he crossed paths with Fortune and her associates is intriguing although it cannot yet be proved. Almost certainly he could have been aware of them through reading Fortune's and Seymour's articles in the Society's magazine or in the British journal *The Occult Review*.

Like Dion Fortune, Gardner found it wisest to write about what he learned at first in the form of fiction. His novel about Witchcraft, *High Magic's Aid*, was published in 1949, followed only later by nonfiction books such as *Witchcraft Today* in 1954 and *The Meaning of Witchcraft* in 1959. What had changed in the meantime was the law. Until 1951, it was illegal in England to say one was practicing Witchcraft, thanks to the Witchcraft Act of 1735. (The act had modified an earlier harsher law; after 1735 witchcraft was no longer a hanging offense.) The law was repealed in 1951, however, after lobbying by Spiritualist churches. The last trial under the Witchcraft Act had been that of a Spiritualist medium in 1944 whose "crime" was revealing, allegedly through her mediumistic channeling of a dead British sailor, that his ship had been sunk earlier by the Germans. This revelation came days before the government officially said the ship was lost, so the medium, Helen Duncan, was chiefly guilty of embarrassing the wartime bureaucrats.

With the Witchcraft Act repealed, Gardner and other British witches could go public. (It is important to understand that Gardner never claimed that his coven and what became the "Gardnerian" tradition of Witchcraft were the only representatives of British Wicca.) His coven, however, split over inevitable internal disagreements about how much publicity was good and how much was harmful, according to Doreen Valiente, who had been initiated by Gardner in 1953.

The birth of Gardnerian Witchcraft was flavored by World War II. For example, shortly after the war ended Gardner and his associates produced the the "Witch Laws"—which supposedly had been handed down since the persecutions of the 1300s-1600s. Almost half of the 162 "verses" are devoted to how to operate covens under persecution. But while the laws are written in pseudo-16th-century English, their outlook more likely reflects the time of Gardner's initiation into Witchcraft on the eve of the Battle of Britain and his experiences during the grim days of 1940 when a German invasion was expected at any time. Living on the southern English coast where an invading army would have landed, Gardner joined the Home Guard, the raggle-taggle body of middle-aged and elderly men prepared to face the German Wehrmacht with shotguns, pistols and pitchforks. At the same time Gardner was moving deeper in Witchcraft, he was preparing for a house-to-house, hedge-to-hedge resistance to the expected German landing. In a letter to the *Daily Telegraph* newspaper, he noted that "Belgium and France were lost because the civilian population bolted instead of staying and delaying the invaders." Because "every free-born Englishman is entitled to have arms to defend himself and his household," he continued, civilians should fight as long as they could.

At the same time, he knew the Home Guard would not hold off German storm troopers for very long. "We expected Hitler on the seashore any day," he later recalled. "We had no weapons worth the name. In my three-mile beach sector there were six shotguns, my

Luger and Donna's (his wife's) revolver, and a few other pistols, with about six rounds apiece for them." For assistance, seven regular British soldiers were also stationed on the three-mile beachfront.

According to Gardner, during the tense summer of 1940 his and other covens performed rituals designed to stop the invasion, and the effort took so much out of them that several elderly coveners died from the stress. The story of the magical operation to stop Hitler, which was said to have peaked at Lammas (the early August festival), became particularly important to British Witches, for it interwove their history with that of the Battle of Britain.

Had an invasion taken place, the next step for the British would have been to form Resistance groups, as occurred in occupied France, Norway, and other countries. Gardner undoubtedly was planning for that step; no wonder so much of his Craft Laws are devoted to organizing secret "cells" of people, providing "safe houses," eluding hostile authorities, resisting torture, and aiding condemned prisoners. But as the Craft Laws were copied and recopied through the 1950s and 1960s by individual Witches, this wartime connection became irrelevant and was lost. In 1971 one version of the laws was published by Llewellyn Publications in *The Book of Shadows*; another version was published in 1969 as part of a biography of the English Witch Alex Sanders. Since then they have been more closely analyzed; in their present form, it is clear that they are not as old as they are made to appear.

But while Gardner, like anyone, was a product of his times, he was also an innovator. He, together with Doreen Valiente and others, took the tradition they had received, blended it with historical records such as Leland's *Aradia*, and made it suitable for their time and ours. Valiente, for example, rewrote some of the Italian invocations Maddalena had given Leland; these proved so successful that they spread to Witches who had no idea of their origin but accepted them as ancient and as representative of what the Old Religion should be—and should have been. (She did, however, ignore Maddalena's material on poisoning evil landlords, destroying the rich through magic, and otherwise carrying out a sort of Renaissance Pagan "liberation theology.")

Still, Gardner, his successors and imitators (such as Alex Sanders ?-1988) were too few for the needs of the times. Particularly in North America there were too many would-be Witches to wait for the slow process of initiatory succession to reach them. Beginning in the late 1960s and early 1970s, these people began to use sources such as Graves's *The White Goddess*, books by Gardner, Valiente and other Witches, and their own psychic guidance to create their own traditions, often flavored by social causes such as feminism (which as Doreen Valiente points out in *The Rebirth of Witchcraft* was overdue in reaching the strict Gardnerian tradition). This do-it-yourself approach was typified by Starhawk's *The Spiral Dance*; its history was chronicled in Margot Adler's *Drawing Down the Moon*.

Some of the established Craft leaders were horrified at these "unauthorized" covens popping up, but the wiser ones eventually saw which way the tide was running and hastened to ride it.

A Word About Tradition

There are magically valid reasons for tradition and initiation. Many Witches do believe that repeating ritual forms builds power and that their spirits do travel more easily where someone earlier has made a way. But at the same time, the Craft looks to Nature (both inner and outer) as its guide and teacher, not to human authority or to a book. (The so-called Book of Shadows is merely a generic term for a Witch's personal ritual handbook; it is not "scripture.") Witches are not asked to refrain from thinking or investigating any matter lest it "harm their faith." Even those who claim traditions independent of Gerald Gardner have adopted his Wiccan Rede (an Old English word meaning counsel or advice): "If it harm none, do what you will." Doing what you will, as the English occultist Aleister Crowley had earlier taught, did not mean "do anything you please" but rather "follow your true spiritual path."

Gardner, incidentally, often wrote "An it harm none ... "; in earlier centuries, "an" also meant "if." He frequently cast his writing on the Craft in mock-archaic language. As with the Craft Laws mentioned above, because he believed he was passing on material whose spirit was old, he probably felt that by using archaic language he was giving it an appropriate "color" as though it had been taken directly from the 16th or 17th centuries, the height of the witchcraft persecutions. If the individual Witch finds this or other archaic-sounding language jarring and not productive of the right emotional effect, he or she should modify it.

Witchcraft, like any other organized activity undertaken by human beings, oscillates between the two poles of "rules" and "inspiration" (or the group and the individual, to put them in different terms). It is likely that we are coming to a time when "tradition" may be gaining a little over individuality, but because it is focused on the small group rather than the large congregation, it is unlikely that the Craft will ever become too bureaucratic. In the small group, the coven, the dynamics of individual relationships are right there for everyone to see, and if a person does not fit in and resonate with the group, he or she will drift away—and, we hope, find the right people to practice with. Likewise, covens "hive off" from each other, which is a normal occurrence and not an expression of failure to stay together.

Individuality will always be important in the Craft, however, because each initiated Witch is a priest or priestess; that is to say, he or she should reach the point of being able to carry out basic ritual and magical work alone or taking his or her place as a leader in the circle. And it is difficult to be an effective magical worker while using forms one does not understand and comprehend emotionally as well as intellectually. For that reason, individual inspiration will always play a major role in Wicca.

In his 1954 book *Witchcraft Today* Gerald Gardner had to be both a historian and an anthropologist. He spoke of the Witches more as "they" than as "we," perhaps because he believed that the entire topic of modern Witchcraft was so startling that it had to be examined at arm's length. This book is different; it is written as "we." And we, as writers, are offering different pathways to participation, from the mysteries of sex magic to the earthly comfort of the old seasonal festivals. If you, the reader, look closely, you may see some small disagreements between different authors' viewpoints, but they will always turn out to be not fundamental differences, but different facets of the same stone.

We believe that the world's need for Witchcraft's wisdom is great, and possibly you will find that you can come home to it as we did. It was always there, like the neglected herbs that keep springing anew in the cracked concrete of a city sidewalk.

SUGGESTIONS FOR FURTHER READING

Adler, Margot. *Drawing Down the Moon*. Boston: Beacon Press, 1987. This is the revised edition, which updates Adler's original 1970s history of American Neopaganism into the 1980s. A unique and valuable book.

Bracelin, J.L. *Gerald Gardner, Witch*. London: Octagon Press, 1960. Although there is some dispute about its authorship, this book remains the only firsthand biography of the man who was instrumental in reviving and recasting the Pagan religion of Witchcraft in the 1940s and 1950s.

Buckland, Raymond. *Buckland's Complete Book of Witchcraft*. St. Paul, Minnesota: Llewellyn Publications, 1986. An extensive handbook on practical Wiccan ritual. It can be effectively paired with the Farrars' book listed below.

Cohn, Norman. *Europe's Inner Demons*. New York: Basic Books, 1975. Subtitled "An Enquiry Inspired by the Great Witch-Hunt," this work by an eminent English historian suggests that the Western collective unconscious has for centuries cherished an idea that somewhere some group of people is meeting at midnight, holding orgies, having sex indiscriminately with each other, and ritually killing the babies that result. The same accusations were made against early Christians by the Romans, against heretics and Jews by the Christians, against medieval and Renaissance "witches" by the Christians, and against so-called "Satanists" today.

Farrar, Janet and Stewart. *The Witches' Way*. London: Robert Hale, 1984. A detailed and comprehensive look at the current form of Gardnerian Witchcraft with a British and Irish emphasis.

Fortune, Dion. *The Sea Priestess*. New York: Samuel Weiser Inc., 1978. First published in 1938, this is one of the 20th century's best magical novels. Its strong Pagan overtones made it commercially unpublishable in the 1930s when it was written despite the success of the author's other books; Fortune had to publish it herself.

Gardner, Gerald. *Witchcraft Today*. Secaucus, New Jersey: Citadel Press, 1973. (Reprint of 1954 edition.)

Ginzburg, Carlo. *The Night Battles*. New York: Penguin, 1985. One of the best scholarly works showing how a "fertility cult" with probable Pagan roots was forced by the Inquisition into its idea of "Satanism."

Graves, Robert. *The White Goddess*. New York: Farrar, Strauss and Giroux, 1966. Despite some gaps in its story, this book has been enormously influential over the last forty-plus years in opening people's minds to the reality of the Goddess. *The White Goddess* is often cited as a key work of "analepsis," the recovering of lost knowledge through intuitive or visionary means.

Harrison, Michael. *The Roots of Witchcraft*. Secaucus, New Jersey: Citadel Press, 1974. Further ideas following Margaret Murray's lead about the Old Religion's survival into the Middle Ages.

Hoyt, Charles Alva. *Witchcraft*. Carbondale, Illinois: Southern Illinois University Press, 1981, 1989. Included here because it summarizes most theories about why the great European witchcraft persecutions occurred. The second edition, published in 1989, is preferable.

Jones, Evan John. *Witchcraft: A Tradition Renewed*. Custer, Washington: Phoenix Publishing, 1990. Together with Doreen Valiente (see below), Jones was a member of an English coven headed by Robert Cochrane (a.k.a. Roy Bowers), a man who claimed to be a hereditary Witch of a non-Gardnerian tradition. Cochrane died in 1966, but Jones believes his system was an authentic reconstruction and here describes it. Valiente supplies a lengthy preface.

Leland, Charles G. *Aradia, or The Gospel of the Witches*. London: David Nutt, 1899. Leland, an American folklorist, found evidence of surviving organized Pagan practice in northern Italy in the 1890s. Much of what Leland discovered was absorbed by British Witchcraft in the 1950s.

Levy, G. Rachel. *The Gate of Horn*. London: Faber and Faber, 1948. Subtitled "A study of the religious conceptions of the Stone Age, and their influence upon European thought," this was another groundbreaking work on our Pagan roots.

Murray, Margaret A. *The Witch-cult in Western Europe*. Oxford: Clarendon Press, 1921. This was the first of three books written by the English archaeologist arguing that the Old Religion persisted (with royal patronage at least through the 12th century) into the Middle Ages. It was followed by *The God of the Witches* and *The Divine King in England*.

Rose, Elliot. *A Razor for a Goat: A Discussion of Certain Problems in the History of Witchcraft and Diabolism*. Toronto: University of Toronto Press, 1962. This Canadian historian examined Margaret Murray's evidence for the Old Religion's survival and concluded that she had bent the facts to fit her theories.

Seymour, Charles R.F. *The Forgotten Mage*. Wellingborough, Northhamptonshire: The Aquarian Press Ltd., 1986. Edited by Dolores Ashcroft-Nowicki, this collection of Seymour's essays on the Western Mystery Tradition is the best bridge between Witchcraft and ceremonial magic. Seymour not only comprehended the esoteric history of the West, he understood and worked with the rising Pagan currents.

Starhawk. *The Spiral Dance*. San Francisco: Harper and Row, 1979. A significant handbook of do-it-yourself Witchcraft in North America.

Valiente, Doreen. *The Rebirth of Witchcraft*. London: Robert Hale Ltd., 1989. Initiated by Gerald Gardner, Valiente created much of the ritual used today by Witches who have hardly heard of her. She has also researched the existence of the "New Forest Coven" of the 1930s which Gardner joined.

An Insider's Look at Pagan Festivals

by Oz

A huge cone of firewood stood expectantly in the center of the ceremonial area, which slowly filled with hundreds of dark, robed figures, shadowy in the late twilight. I stood near the back of the crowd, carrying a very tired 2-year-old on my hip. I caught glimpses of priestesses and priests moving in the center of the giant ring of people and could barely make out their words. Their invocations sounded distant as though I were eavesdropping on a circle existing in another time which I could not clearly see or hear. I lost all sense of time's passage. My mind wandered; my eyes drifted over the hooded shapes. Nothing distinguished the eon or locale. It could have been any time, any place. I was aware of movement in each of the four cardinal directions and occasionally heard the crowd call in unison, "Blessed be."

Then from nowhere torches appeared above the heads of people in front of me, and there was a deep heavy silence. I knew, although I could not see, that the fire was being lit. Again, any sense of time slipped away.

Suddenly the entire woodpile was aflame with giant fingers leaping and crackling in the night sky, sparks flying upwards. Just as suddenly, the amorphous crowd became a raging, moving, encircling current. I jumped backwards to avoid being swept away by those rushing past, some holding hands and forming long snakes of people, others whirling themselves about and weaving in and out between the others, many shouting and leaping in the air. Everyone chanted; drums beat loudly; the fire's heat stung my face. I looked down into the amazed eyes of my small daughter, who clung to me tightly. Tears ran down my face. I felt a tremendous emotion as though after a long search I had finally found my people again.

The year was 1979, the place the first large Pagan festival I had attended, set in rural Indiana. Nevertheless, I knew the place, the fire, the dance, the night. I had been here before in other times and other lands—in other lives.

Almost as soon as Witches and Pagans began to reappear, they began to gather again. At first the meetings were small and secretive. In the 1950s Witches emerged from tightly-knit covens and family groups, and the first books about modern Witchcraft emerged. In the 1960s the traditional groups grew in size, and new traditions were born. More books appeared, and the very first Pagan newsletters were exchanged. In the 1970s, some few dared hold conferences, seminars and "open" circles. The fears from memories of persecution died slowly, however, and the first semi-public meetings were marked by caution. Some Witches were afraid to share their rites with others, and most simply did not attend at all. Gradually, curiosity and confidence spread throughout the Witches' world, and once-small meetings snowballed into sizable events. Along with so much else of the ways of old, the Witches' Meet was being reborn in a new and vital form.

By the 1980s, the Witch's bookshelf was full of titles on dozens of topics. Stores in every major metropolis catered to Witches' needs. Local, national and international newsletters abounded, and even Pagan and Wiccan computer networks were created. Most significantly, a Pagan could travel across the United States and Canada, to Ireland and Britain, other parts of Europe, or even Australia, and find gatherings of like-minded folk: Witches meeting merrily, exchanging ideas, talents, rituals, music, traditions, inspirations, and love for the Goddesses and Gods (as well as one another). As rounds of "Give Me that Ol' Time Religion" and "We Won't Wait Any Longer" were heard in the woods, something was stirring, alive again and growing. "The Goddess is Alive and Magic is Afoot" became the chanted byword for new generations of the Craft of the Wise.

Today's Paganism has grown from seeds of awareness kept alive since ancestral times. It responds to deep cultural yearnings for something relevant and "connected," a gut feeling for what life is really about. The awe I have seen in the eyes of a white man watching the sacred Indian dances at Taos Pueblo is an awe based in envy: we crave ceremony, ritual and magic in our sterile modern lives. These cravings, these natural spiritual impulses have led to Wicca and Paganism's resurgence. Many people have come back to the woods and to the tribal gatherings, looking for something—perhaps something they remember deep inside.

Today they find many types of Pagan gatherings and festivals: retreats, seminars, training sessions, extended workshops, one-day gatherings, local events and large festivals that can range from a few days to a week long and from 100 to 500 in attendance. Locations vary from hotels to camps to wilderness and the facilities available from plenty to none. Gatherings come in different "flavors." In Britain and elsewhere in Europe they are a more recent development than in the United States and consequently more traditional in form; in the U.S. and to some extent Australia the emphasis is more on diversity and experimentation. Different U.S. regions have particular styles as well; thus, a gathering in the Northeast may be distinct from one in the Midwest or Southwest. But wherever Pagans assemble, a different standard of social norms and reality-consensus is adopted, one which is more open to alternative forms of self-expression and states of existence.

The first printed notices of these events in Pagan newsletters and magazines are usually sketchy; one gets more information by writing to the sponsors. For security reasons, maps and final directions are only sent to those who have paid their registration fees. Pagans disavow the idea of charging large sums for spiritual teaching; our get-togethers are priced modestly, and in most cases special arrangements are possible for those who cannot afford the fees.

A festival-goer's motto might well be, "Be prepared for anything." Dress, weather permitting, is often "clothing optional," meaning that outfits may cover all, any or no parts of the body—anything from paint, glitter and feathers to elaborate costumes or casual, ordinary dress. But underneath the hedonism, the free-wheeling environment, and social experimentation common at Pagan gatherings lies real sensitivity and caring. What looks like decadence and laid-back living is only a veneer over a sincere exploration of group and neo-tribal morality.

This is not to say there are no conflicts: for example, between those who wish to stay up all night drumming and those who crave a quiet night's sleep. More serious infringements on personal safety and privacy—usually the result of persons taking advantage of the festival's liberal atmosphere—have generally been dealt with effectively by the communities themselves. At some events, social and sexual behavior options have been discussed openly. I participated in one such discussion where those present ranged in age from late teens to late middle age and included self-acknowledged gay men, lesbians, heterosexuals, bisexuals, monogamists, polygamists, celibates and those both promiscuous and picky. The conversation was on both how to communicate and how to act on one's preferred sexual style in such a multi-optioned environment, but generally everyone agreed that any act or expression that failed to honor another's right to his or her own preferences was unacceptable.

Children too are more and more part of Pagan gatherings. There may be planned children's ceremonies, activities and cooperative childcare. Festivals are also popular places for handfastings (Pagan weddings) and coming-of-age ceremonies. Other activities may include bonfires, drumming sessions, dancing and spontaneous theater.

One thing almost certain to be present is music: original, creative earth-root songs, ballads and canticles sung to the Gods, Goddesses and spirits of all kinds, songs of magic, nature and humor. Pagans love to sing, play all kinds of instruments, and jam. Larger gatherings will include bardic circles and talent shows with poetry, story-telling and stand-up Pagan comedy. I have even seen a professional magic strip act.

Workshops are always part of a festival, scheduled and unscheduled and ranging broadly in variety and quality. Topics extend from runes to radionics, the use of Tarot in psychotherapy to "kitchen tricks for sabbats," qabalistic totem animals and shamanic drum-making. Pagan craftspersons and merchants are always present; the festival is one place to find handcrafted swords,

Photo © 1991 Malcolm Brenner / Eyes Open

wands and crowns as well as dream-pillows, pre-consecrated candles and potholders embroidered with pentagrams.

Not every event is serious. Silliness is sacred to many Pagans and manifests through such events as the "Boston tea party" originally hosted by Athanor, a Pagan group from Massachusetts, at one festival. Everyone is encouraged to dress in wigs, corsets, black lace stockings, fluffy nighties, lace teddies and other lingerie for an afternoon or evening of raucous rock and rollin'. While satirizing Madison Avenue images of sexuality, these functions provide great ways to release inhibitions and act out exhibitionist fantasies in a safe environment. Soon after the first "tea party," nearly every Pagan gathering in the U.S. had its own variation, from Ragnar's Pub in Georgia to the Disco Tipi in New Mexico.

While at one time Wicca and other Pagan traditions were fertility religions, concerned with crops and herds and babies, today the fertility magic is directed towards the development of the self and toward one's environment. At a festival this fertility is actualized by the shared insights, stimulation and opportunities provided by the special setting and other people. The outcome is change and transformation of the minds, realities and experience of the participants. The feeling of "I am not alone," the inhibitions that might be shed with clothing, the ecstasy of abandonment to the dance around the fire are all experiences that can lead to subtle but profound changes in individuals who can acknowledge and integrate them.

Here lies the true magic of a Pagan festival; in these experiences true spirituality is found—especially if "spirit" is seen to encompass that sense of life and vivacity included in the broader definition of the word. I have seen partakers of festival mysteries in tears at every gathering I ever attended, recounting the wonder of their own experiences. I remember well a vision that came to one woman at a gathering, directing her to a life work with dolphins and other animals, a dream that is now coming true.

The focus of most major gatherings is ritual. Much of Paganism's greatest growth in recent years has been through the sharing and performing of large rites and ceremonies. Twenty years ago a high priestess might need to know how to perform the traditional rites for her own coven and train others to do the same. Today some Pagan clergy have learned how to choreograph rites that are effective for several hundred people at a time as well as how to integrate the ideas of diverse traditions into one cohesive ceremony. We have gone from simply performing traditional coven ritual in front of large groups to developing elaborate rites befitting new occasions, circumstances and contributors. This process continues to evolve with every season showing new ventures into festival ritual that reflect the ongoing search for more creativity and meaning.

A tremendous example of multi-group ritual which I will never forget took place at the 1983 Pagan Spirit Gathering in Wisconsin under a full Moon in June, conceived and directed by my good friend Peter. Its creation required the talents of more than thirty people, and it was one of the first festival rites I had participated in that was entirely designed and performed on-site, requiring several days of rehearsals and costuming searches.

It began with the entrance of two half-naked men, one black and one white, who shouldered a litter bearing a prone and very pregnant woman, her breasts and belly painted with brilliant red spirals. The three of them formed a symbolic gateway of birth through which each person entered the ritual circle by passing under the litter. Everyone joined in the chant, "And the full Moon is Her vagina spread wide. And the full Moon is Her vagina spread wide, with the wild realm of all possibilities, every possibility, pouring out," repeating the melody in a hypnotic rhythm.

Then followed the invocations of the Goddesses, thirteen in all, including an Amazon warrior, the Earth Mother herself, She-Who-Loves-Women, and others. One by one, each was called to the circle, entering with the performance designed to evoke the nature of the Goddess represented. Kali danced in to a heavy Eastern drumbeat, writhing beautifully beneath the sword balanced on Her head. Hekate, dark and hooded, threatened dramatically with Her staff as she whirled about the circle.

And then entered Discordia, not to be forgotten Goddess of all that might and thus will go wrong. She appeared with a huge, completely veiled head, carrying a large "boom box" cassette recorder. Setting it down, she punched buttons for several seconds with no result. She slammed the side of the box—still nothing. And then someone in the crowd yelled, "Hail, Discordia!" honoring the by now quite apparent manifest presence of the Goddess who was obviously letting Herself be known in the usual manner. The crowd laughed wholeheartedly; the tape player was replaced by a working one and the man playing Discordia proceeded to reveal a huge Bugs Bunny mask beneath the veil while dancing to the recording of the Looney Toons theme song.

Next to be invoked was Diana, played by a beautiful young woman wearing only metallic gold paint from the waist up. She strode elegantly into the circle, followed by her back-up vocalists, who broke into a Paganized version of Diana Ross's "Ain't No Mountain High Enough." Suitable for a modern Charge of the Goddess, the words ran, "If you need me, call me, no matter where you are, no matter how far. Just call my name, and I'll be there, in a hurry—on that you can depend and never worry."

Gods too were invoked in a flaming dance with lit sparklers. Finally the Goddesses handed out seeds to everyone, and these were charged with the intention to make a positive change in each person's everyday life. The seeds were planted, symbolically and actually, and fertilized by the creativity that had been invoked.

Because of the festival circuit, life-long friendships, new partnerships, new covens and new projects have been conceived. The circuit carries the new oral traditions of the Craft: chants, songs, legends, ceremonies and even sometimes politics and newer levels of consciousness. Every year new songs and lyrics spread from one festival to another. I remember well one year when these words could be heard in Pagan circles from California to New York: "We are an old people. We are a new people. We are the same people, stronger than before." That summer it was as though we were all remembering something together.

At the first gatherings, some of the excitement came from witnessing the novelty and variety: new ways to invoke the Goddess, new styles of ritual dress, variations on ritual methods. This excitement will continue as long as there are newcomers to the festivals. Those of us with so many seasons and events behind us have seen the melding and blending of our diverse ways. Inevitably in the course of human affairs cultural and religious diversity is sacrificed as people become intermixed. This is not altogether negative because it offers the opportunity for mutual growth. Because so many Craft traditions suffered at the hands of those in charge for centuries, and because our worship is at its best as a living practice, it may be that these new bursts of creativity will redeem what remains of our ancestors' ways. We may not wind the Maypole as was done hundreds of years ago but we are winding it with a spirit from and for our own times. Our challenge is to continue developing new forms and new traditions while maintaining the all-important sense of awe and mystery, never losing sight of that which is sacred.

The forms that Pagan gatherings of the future will take depend on the directions being chosen today. There have been obstacles, including misunderstanding and harassment from society at large such as that created by the current paranoia about Satanism. But internal strife, backbiting and gossip have plagued both the events and their organizers and coordinators, often more ferociously than any outside interference. And yet the movement continues. As our entire world is swept up in the tides preceding the transition into the Aquarian Age, we find ourselves surrounded by changing culture and con- sciousness. The Craft, ancient as it may be, has come alive again just in time to participate in this great transforma- tion. Wicca's part in planetary spiritual evolution will depend on the real magical work done at Pagan gather- ings today. Through social experimentation, personal transformation and consciousness exploration, Pagans are in the forefront of the process. Whether or not they will be able to share what they are learning with the world around them remains to be seen. Our festivals could have important social and spiritual implications— or they could be seen as just another minor aberration in humanity's history.

There is much to speculate, meditate and divine upon. Perhaps the Witches really have been reincarnated in these times to work together again. We come to these gatherings looking for our roots, friends we have known before, those we feel called to be with in this life, or just a sense of direction and belonging. Many have found what they looked for and gone on to pursue new and old dreams and projects. Others keep the festival fires alive, helping shape the ideas, enjoyments, lessons and connections that shape Witchcraft today. There is a spark alive in the Craft that has kept it from dying out and that is the spark of Desire. Our own Goddess tells us, "I am that which is attained at the end of Desire." It is this Desire that leads our circles and dances in ever ongoing cycles. The very fact that the ancient worship of Nature survived in Western culture throughout centuries of repression and persecution itself represents an important link between human consciousness and the consciousness of the Earth. None of us can any longer hold a worldview separate from all other living beings around us, either as a race apart from the animals, seas, forests and jungles or as Witches separate from outsiders. We *are* one planet, one people. Humans are coming to understand this as tolerance increases for ideas once stamped out because they did not fit with the egocentric cultural goals of former times. The old religions that remember the ways of balance with Nature re-emerge in these times. And we have to ask ourselves, "Why? Is it only so that we may continue our individual evolutions, or is there something vitally important that Witches and Pagans have to share?"

ABOUT THE AUTHOR

Oz is co-founder of the Wiccan-based tradition Children of the Dawn, conceived in the late 1960s. She is responsible for numerous Pagan happenings in her home state of New Mexico, where she also materializes stories about Witchcraft and the mystic arts for television, newspapers and radio. She has spoken about the Craft before high school, university and general audiences as well as other religious groups. The channeling, designing, and facilitation of ceremonies for every aspect of human desire is her special avocation. In her work she has sought to bring real transformational magick into the sacred circle of celebratory rites. Her ritual adventurings at Pagan festivals and elsewhere have included the deeply spiritual as well as the enigmatic and not-so-sublime, ranging from impregnation of the Earth with actual thought to initiations with cashew nuts. Today she combines her interest and studies in Native Ways, Wicca and Hermetic Magick with ongoing work as priestess to Hekate, goddess of magick. She is currently writing a book about ceremony and in her spare time likes to read dictionaries of dead languages.

Seasonal Rites / Magical Rites

by Pauline Campanelli

Witchcraft is a religion whose essence is rooted in Neolithic shamanism. Through ritual celebration of seasonal changes Witches attune themselves to the creative forces of the Cosmos. Our rituals are based on fragments of ancient practices, some preserved by tradition and some adopted from other sources. And while Witches celebrate in groups—covens—a great number practice their religion alone, and our rituals can be adapted to fit either circumstance.

Witchcraft shares with ancient shamanism the fundamental belief that all of Nature is a manifestation of the Gods and that therefore everything has a spirit. We are not separate from Nature nor "above" it, but are a part of it. Witchcraft is a "polytheistic" religion in that Witches worship many aspects of divinity under different names, but in reality all gods are one God, all goddesses one Goddess. It is a religion of duality or polarity, recognizing that the creative process results from the interaction of opposites—positive and negative, male and female, spirit and matter, God and Goddess—but not "good and evil," evil being the result of a cosmic imbalance. Most Witches believe in reincarnation and the natural cycles of birth, death and rebirth as expressed in Nature by the changing seasons of the wheel of the year.

Witches celebrate the changing seasons at the solstices, equinoxes and at the midpoints between them ("cross-quarter days") with festivals called sabbats. Regardless of the season, sabbat celebrations traditionally begin with the same opening ritual.

The ritual takes place in a circle, which again by tradition is nine feet in diameter. (Larger or smaller circles are used depending on the number of participants and space available.)

The circle must have an altar—a small wooden table is ideal. The altar is placed at the northern point of the circle or, depending on the tradition followed, in the east, facing the rising Sun and Moon. On the altar will be the following: a pair of candles, a pentacle, the book of rituals, a cup of wine or fruit juice, the ritual knife (athame) of each person participating, a wand, a plate of cakes, and objects representing the four magical elements—an incense burner for Air, a bowl of water for Water, a red candle for Fire, and a bowl of salt for Earth.

There might also be figures representing aspects of the God and Goddess while some Witchcraft traditions add a sword, a scourge, a bell, a broom or a cauldron. The circle itself would have been previously decorated according to the season with flowers, leaves, fruits, etc., and a candle placed at the four compass points. Another useful accessory is a tape recorder to play music during the ritual unless one of the coveners is a musician.

Once all is ready the priestess and priest enter the circle. One of them may signal the ritual's beginning by ringing a clear-toned bell. The priestess then begins by placing her athame's point into the bowl of water and saying words like:

> *Creature of water, cast out from these all negativity and limitations of the material world. In the name of the Mother Goddess and the Horned God do I exorcise thee, O Creature of Water.*[1]

Then the priest purifies the salt by placing his athame's point in it and saying words like:

> *Blessings upon this salt: may all negative influence be cast out and all good enter herein. I bless thee that thou mayest aid me in the ancient Craft, in the name of the Mother Goddess and the Horned God.*

(The actual names that the coven uses would be substituted here.)

He then pours some of the salt into the water.

Taking her athame or the ritual sword, the priestess draws the circle with its point to the floor, moving sunwise (clockwise or "deosil") from the northern point. Coveners have been waiting outside the circle at the eastern point; now the priestess makes a "doorway" by raising the athame to the height of a person, drawing it across for two or three feet and then back down to the floor. As she inscribes the circle she and the coveners visualize a bright blue flame emanating from the athame's point and making the circle.

Then the priestess invites each covener in through the "doorway," alternating men and women, after which the door is closed by her redrawing that portion of the circle. With all participants inside, the circle is consecrated by the priestess walking its circumference and sprinkling it with the salted water, followed by the priest with the incense. Next the priestess states:

> *I conjure thee a circle of power, that thou art a boundary between the world of men and the realm of the mighty gods. In the name of the Mother Goddess and the Horned God do I consecrate this circle of power!*

During the consecration, the circle has been walked three times—with the blade, the salted water and the incense—but in fact it has been consecrated in all four elements. The incense symbolized Air, the salted water both Earth and Water, and the blade symbolized the Fire in which it was formed.

To complete the consecration the priestess walks to the eastern point and facing east she draws a pentagram in the air with her athame, speaking words such as:

> *I invite ye Guardians of the East whose element is Air. Bring to this circle the breath of life. Witness these rites and guard this circle.*

The same invocation is made at the other three quarters, substituting the words "South whose element is Fire," "West ... Water" and "North ... Earth." The priestess finishes by returning to the eastern point and saluting it.

Now the priest and priestess might purify one another by dipping their fingers in the salted water and anointing one another, each drawing the pentagram on the other's chest, saying words like:

> *With this water art thou purified and fit to serve the gods.*

Then the priest will anoint each of the women in the coven in a like manner, and the priestess will anoint the men.

Now the priest kneels before the priestess and performs a ritual known as "Drawing Down the Moon," inviting the Goddess to descend upon the priestess who then, acting as the Goddess, recites what is called the "Charge of the Goddess":

> *Listen to the words of the Great Mother, she who of old was also called among men Artemis, Astarte, Athene, Dione, Melusine, Aphrodite, Cerridwen, Dana, Arianrhod, Isis, Bride[2], and by many other names. Whenever ye have need of any thing, once in the month, and better it be when the Moon is full, then shall ye assemble in some secret place and adore the spirit of me, who am Queen of all witcheries.*

Following the Charge the priest gives the priestess the fivefold kiss. He begins by kissing each foot, saying, "Blessed are thy feet which have brought thee in these ways." At the knees: "Blessed are thy knees which kneel at the sacred altar." At the womb: "Blessed is thy womb without which we would not be." At the breasts: "Blessed are thy breasts formed in beauty and in strength." At the lips: "Blessed are thy lips which shall utter the sacred names."

Then if the coven truly believes in the polarity of God and Goddess, the Horned God is invoked and asked to descend upon the priest, while the priestess returns the fivefold kiss.

Finally, the music begins, and priestess leads the coven in a dance deosil (sunwise) about the circle. The music's tempo and volume gradually increase; faster and faster the Witches dance. As they dance the power of magic is generated, faster and faster, round and round, until the priestess—sensing enough power has been raised—signals a stop.

From this point on the ritual varies according to the season. In many Craft traditions, the wheel of the year begins at Halloween, often called by the old Celtic name of Samhain.[3]

Here begins the year's darkest time, midway between the autumn equinox and the winter solstice. It is a time when the spirit world is close to the world of the living, and the veil between the two is thin. For this reason Witches celebrate the Samhain sabbat by inviting the spirits of the deceased to join us. The circle might be decorated with pumpkins, gourds and autumn leaves, especially oak leaves that symbolize the Lord of Death. The candles at the four directions might be placed in jack-o-lanterns and a "gateway" left at the western point—the direction of death—through which the dead may enter. The spirits are invited during the rite, which may include a spiral dance danced counter-clockwise ("widdershins"), symbolic of rebirth. Some device for communicating with the dead such as a Ouija board might be in the circle. At Samhain Witches hope to receive messages not only from recently deceased loved ones, but from predecessors in the Craft, their Pagan ancestors or kindred spir-

Illustration of Samhain by Dan Campanelli from **Ancient Ways**
by Pauline Campanelli (Llewellyn Publications)

its. This is also a time for predicting the future by casting runes or reading the Tarot cards. The Goddess is honored in her aspect as The Crone, the Goddess of the Dark Mysteries. The God is honored in his aspect as the Horned God of the Dead, not only of humans but of animals as well.

Yule, falling on December 21, the winter solstice, is the next sabbat. The days begin growing longer and the dark period begins to lessen. To Witches, now comes the birth of the Divine Child, the new solar year.

The Yule circle might be adorned with holly and oak, symbolic of the waning and waxing Sun, and evergreen boughs symbolic of rebirth. To celebrate the waxing Sun a Yule log is traditionally burned and its ashes kept as amulets of protection and fertility. The God is honored in his aspect as Divine Child and the Goddess as the Divine Mother.

On the night of February 1 Witches celebrate the Imbolc[4] sabbat. This night, halfway between the winter solstice and the vernal (spring) equinox is the time when Nature begins to stir unseen and awaken from winter's death-like sleep.

The circle might be adorned with white flowers: snowdrops, Christmas roses or paper whites—or not adorned at all, symbolizing Nature's apparent barrenness at this time. The ritual might include lighting many candles to symbolize the Sun's increasing light. Many Witches also perform a rite called "Bride's bed," which consists of dressing a doll made with corn or other grain and placing it in a basket with a wand representing the God. The Goddess is honored at this sabbat as the Corn Maiden and the God is honored as the Spirit Father.

**Illustration of Yule by Dan Campanelli from Ancient Ways
by Pauline Campanelli (Llewellyn Publications)**

On or about March 21 Witches celebrate the vernal equinox, sometimes called Ostara. This is the time when night and day, dark and light, are equal, and the light begins to grow greater than the dark. The circle might be decorated with spring flowers—daffodils, tulips, hyacinths, pussy willows—or bowls and baskets of colored eggs. This is the time for the ritual blessing of seeds, and as they did in ancient times, Witches make offerings to the Goddess with colored eggs and cakes, sometimes inscribed with solar crosses. At this sabbat the Goddess is honored in her aspect as the Maiden and the God as her brother/consort the Sun God.

The eve of May 1 is Beltaine, along with Samhain one of the most sacred days in the Witches' calendar. The circle is decorated with spring flowers, especially wild ones. During the ritual a May Queen is crowned with chaplet of flowers and a May King is crowed with a wreath of green leaves. A Maypole, symbolizing the phallus that gives the spark of life, is danced around and entwined with ribbons, while a fire made with nine woods is kindled to celebrate the strengthening of the Sun. The Goddess is honored at Beltaine in her aspect as the White Goddess of fertility and the God as the Lord of the Greenwood. Beltaine is the celebration of the Divine Marriage.

On about June 21, the longest day of the year, is the celebration of Midsummer, the summer solstice. Magical herbs such as St. John's wort and vervain are traditionally gathered now. The circle might be adorned with summer flowers—sunflowers are ideal. On this day bonfires are lit to celebrate the Sun at the peak of its power. Witches leap over the flames and make amulets of rowan or rue to hang in homes and barns for the protection of animals.

A Celebration of the Harvest *by Dan Campanelli from* **Wheel of the Year** *by Pauline Campanelli (Llewellyn Publications)*

The God is honored in his aspect as the Sun God and the Goddess as the Earth Mother.

The eve of August 1 is Lammas[5], the celebration of the first harvest. The circle is adorned with ears of corn, baskets of vegetables and reaping tools. The ritual itself is a thanksgiving for the harvest, particularly the grain harvest, and ritual eating and sharing of bread and wine is the sabbat's main theme. At Lammas Witches honor the Goddess in her aspect as all-providing Earth Mother, Grain Goddess or Corn Mother, and the God is honored as the sacrificed God of Grain.

September 21 is the autumn equinox when day and night are of equal length, and the hours of the night begin to grow longer than those of day. The circle is adorned with autumn leaves, seed pods and fall fruits. Witches prepare to bid farewell to the Maiden of Spring and the Mother of Summer, and as nature prepares for the death-like sleep of winter, Witches welcome the Crone and honor the God in his aspect as God of the dying Sun, the God of death and rebirth.

When the seasonal portion of any sabbat rite is completed, the priest takes the cup of wine in his hands and offers it to the priestess. She raises her athame in her clasped hands and places its point in the wine, saying words like:

> *As the cup is to the Female, so the athame is to the male. United they become One.*

Then the priest consecrates the wine, pours a libation to the Gods and shares the rest among the coveners. The priestess does likewise with the plate of cakes. Now is a time for merriment, for telling tales and playing games, as the Witches relax and rejoice within the circle. When the sabbat has ended, the Goddess and God are solemnly thanked for their sacred presence. Then the priestess goes to each of the four compass points and, using her athame, draws the pentagram in the reverse order to which she drew it originally, thanking the guardians of the four directions for their protection. The candles are extinguished, again in reverse order from the way they were lit, and the Witches bid each other, "Merry meet, merry part and merry meet again!"

Aside from the eight major sabbats, Witches customarily also meet monthly, usually during the full Moon. These meetings are called "esbats" and their purpose is for working magic. Witchcraft is an ancient religion that celebrates the year's changing seasons but it is also a religion of magic.

The magic worked could be for a variety of reasons: to heal a sick friend or to help someone to have success in some undertaking. But no matter what kind of magic is being worked, it is never done with out the permission of the recipient. Magic is never worked to harm anyone, since Witches believe that any harm done magically is returned threefold. There are hundreds of charms and spells for protection, prosperity, love and success. And there are thousands of variations with herbs, candles, spells and knots. Most Witches create their own charms or spells based on ancient traditions. (See "Witchcraft and Healing" for examples.)

The esbat's opening and closing rituals are similar to those of the seasonal sabbat, and the magic's results are often amazing. But of far greater importance to Witches than working spells is venerating the ancient Gods. By aligning ourselves with Nature's creative forces, by celebrating the seasonal changes of the Wheel of the Year, we seem to move effortlessly toward our goals and our Gods.

ABOUT THE AUTHOR

Pauline Campanelli and her husband Dan have been practicing Wiccans for more than two decades. Because of their deep religious beliefs, they have evolved a lifestyle based on natural magic. In their 18th-century home in New Jersey's Delaware Valley magic is a part of their everyday life.

Pauline and Dan are also author and illustrator of *Wheel of the Year* (Llewellyn Publications, 1989) and *Ancient Ways: Reclaiming Pagan Traditions* (1991). Their new book, *Circles, Groves and Sanctuaries*, is expected to be released in 1992. They have contributed articles and artwork to such publications as *Circle Network News*, *FATE Magazine*, *Llewellyn's 1991 Magical Almanac*, Alan Vaughan's *Incredible Coincidence*, Joan Bingham and Dolores Riccio's *Haunted Houses: U.S.A.*, and Elizabeth Pepper and John Wilcock's *Witches' Almanac* (1991).

Both Pauline and Dan are professional artists, he working in watercolors and she in oils. Their home and artwork have been featured in *Colonial Homes* and *Country Living* magazines and on a program produced on their art and lives by New Jersey Network for the Public Broadcasting System. Prints of their paintings are available throughout the United States and Europe.

NOTES

[1] The precise wording will vary according to the coven. Some will substitute the more modern "you" for the old second-person pronouns "thou" and "thee."

[2] Pronounced in Irish as "Breed."

[3] Pronounced in Irish Gaelic as "*sow*-in" and in Scottish Gaelic as "*sav*-en."

[4] Pronounced in Irish as "im-*mol'g*." In some traditions it is called Oimelc.

[5] From the Old English "loaf mass," a grain-harvest festival.

Witchcraft and Healing

by Morwyn

It is an unwritten law of Wicca that Witches be healers. In former times they were the herbalists, the Old Wives to whom country folk, villagers and city dwellers alike flocked for cures for what ailed them. This commitment to healing continues in contemporary Witchcraft and is one of the Craft's most appealing aspects to modern seekers of spiritual enlightenment.

As Witches, we hold that humankind is an integral part of nature and that physical, mental and spiritual ills may be reflections of personal imbalances in relationship to the universe. Consequently, the Craft's approach to healing encompasses the whole person. This view explains why natural healing agents—herbs, for example—are used in spells that go beyond a physical, medicinal level into areas such as love, wealth, protection, spiritual enhancement and so on.

Likewise, divination, or seeing into possible futures using cards, the "magic mirror," crystal ball, pendulum or astrology, stems from the Witch's desire to help others to chose from potential options and thus be able to live their lives better. We do this as part of a larger effort to attune our bodies, minds and spirits to the universal energy pulses known as cosmic tides, aided by meditation, seasonal rituals, solar and lunar rites. Without this attunement, the Witch lacks the equilibrium necessary to aid others from a balanced position of strength.

Two modern movements mesh well with Witchcraft's traditional use of herbs and psychic healing methods. From an environmental point of view, herbs and other natural materials are "renewable resources." Researching healing herbs and saving herbal knowledge for posterity are enormously important to the welfare of the majority of Earth's inhabitants who cannot afford "standard" medical care and expensive manufactured remedies.

Second, many people, particularly women, have come to view our medical establishment as physically, socially and politically manipulative and interventionist, and are striving to take control of their own bodies.[1] Instead, they want to help themselves in natural ways over which they themselves hold power.

Psychic Diagnosis of Disease

Modern Witches use a variety of methods to diagnose and treat illness. One very ancient method still in use is astrology, which permits the healer to become familiar with the patient's inherent tendencies towards particular diseases.

Once scorned by many outside the Craft as atavistic mumbo-jumbo, astrology is a compendium of wisdom amassed over the ages and reflecting centuries of human beings' total experience. It is based on the "doctrine of signatures,"[2] which states that each heavenly body is linked to an aspect of life on Earth. For example, Venus is associated with love, friendship, harmony, beauty and pleasure. Mars represents strength, warfare, athletics and sexual drive. Neptune is connected with dreams, the occult and the unconscious mind.

Astrology divides humanity into twelve basic character types, represented by the signs of the zodiac. Each type is viewed as prone to specific physical and psychological maladies. For example, Gemini is associated with lung problems such as asthma.

The Witch may also read the patient's "aura" to help with diagnosis. Certain sensitive people claim to be able to perceive an emanation like light around the body, particularly the head, which can have different colors and shadings. Aura-seers say that diseased areas seem to bulge or exhibit dark patches or other discolorations.

Some Witches use "pallomancy," divination by pendulum, to diagnose disease. Any favorite small object such as a crystal, stone, necklace or ring is suspended by a thread or lightweight chain so that it hangs down about twelve inches.

To try this method, hold the chain between your fingers and program the pendulum by willing it to swing one way for "yes" and another way for "no," either side-to-side or to-and-fro.

Have the patient lie comfortably face up on a bed or the floor while you move the pendulum slowly up and down his or her body at a distance of about a foot, stopping every few inches to ask whether this is the location of the malady until the pendulum gives a "yes" answer.

According to dowsers (people adept with pendulums and similar devices), the answer is gained in one of two ways. Either the dowser unconsciously gathers information from the patient and translates it into pendulum movements, or he or she delves into the depths of his or her own psyche to the Higher Self, then transmits knowledge gained there via the fingers to the pendulum.

Other methods include "psychometry," holding a picture of the patient or an object owned by the patient while gathering impressions, Tarot cards, crystal-gazing, the Ouija board or numerology. Some Witches practice palm reading to diagnose afflictions—a practice confirmed to some degree by traditional science. For instance, it appears that certain lines on the hand presage congenital mental disorders and that some blood cancers also can be detected from the palm. Similarly, there seems to be a physical link between reddish-tinted palms and alcoholism.

Methods of Healing: Chromotherapy

Once a diagnosis is made, the healer decides on a course of treatment. Together with other techniques, many Witches employ "chromotherapy," a treatment dating back to the days of Paracelsus (1493-1531), a Swiss physician of the Renaissance. Its underlying theory that light and color affect all life is amply supported by scientific studies and borne out through natural phenomena such as the time of day that certain flowers open, the way amoebas flee light for darkness, or the fact that human appetites are stimulated by orange and brown-shaded foods.[3]

The human aura is especially sensitive to the color spectrum. Many healers believe that light enters the body at various points along the spinal cord called "chakras," of which there are five or seven, depending on the system used. White light is broken down into the colors of the spectrum, and the vibrations emitted by each color then are distributed to places in the body needing energy. Illness occurs when a blockage forms that impedes the

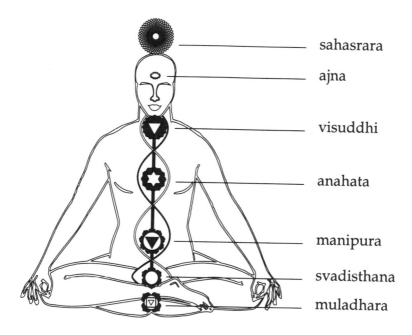

sahasrara

ajna

visuddhi

anahata

manipura

svadisthana

muladhara

The Chakras and the Body

natural movement and absorption of this energy. Psychic healers believe that energy can also leak from a chakra, causing a telltale "discoloration" or deformation of the aura.

To replenish the body's strength, the healer psychically beams into the patient rays of the deficient color, combination of colors or else pure white light (sometimes called astral light). She or he may also bathe the patient in colored light, place the patient in harmonically colored surroundings and/or prescribe a diet of certain colored foods and tinted waters. The patient can continue the therapy by visualizing he or she is breathing in the appropriate colors during meditation.

But Witches also cure by envisioning at a distance the appropriate colors through meditation and ritual. Then they literally will the energies to pass from them through the cosmos and into the patient. The Witch becomes a kind of lightning rod or conductor for the attraction and transmission of cosmic "light." Such healings are often performed by an entire coven during a circle healing rite. Interestingly, when I perform color healings by willing a colored light to penetrate the patient's chakras, I often ask whether the patient can perceive a certain color. I have never had a patient answer incorrectly.

One word of caution: color therapy is based on using the appropriate color(s) and lengths of time for which the patient should be exposed to them. It takes study and practice to be able to administer each color correctly. More often than not, it is the subtle combination of colors manipulated in the right series for the proper length of time that produces the best results. Only a trained color therapist, healer or coven specializing in chromotherapy should attempt to heal with colors.

Herbs in Healing

Early people saw in plants' natural cycles a symbol of life and regeneration. Plants sprouted up seemingly from nowhere, grew, withered and died, only to reappear at the next growing season. Not only did plants seem to embody the secret of reproduction, but when eaten or applied externally, they could bring relief from illnesses, cause pain or pleasure, and even kill.

According to the doctrine of signatures mentioned earlier, plants can be classified according to the zodiac and the planets. Ancient scholars assigned them to their corresponding sign based on their appearance, some salient characteristic or their use. For example, chamomile, which sports a bright, daisy-like flower with white petals radiating from a yellow center, was assigned to the Sun, which in turn was thought to cure sicknesses of the head, eyes and heart, and to dispel melancholy. Likewise, chamomile was taken to alleviate these maladies.

Modern Witches are well aware that herbs taken physically do not necessarily cure according to the doctrine of signatures and consequently their herbal medical prescriptions stem from an empirically tested knowledge of herbs. But at the same time, since a body of lore has evolved on the magical use of herbs, peoples' beliefs have created a kind of magical reality for herbs that is valid in its own right. So when a Witch makes an herbal talisman or sachet for someone to wear, he or she attempts to reach the source of the "dis-ease" on psychic and cosmic levels rather than on the purely physical plane.

Because of this dual approach, herbs possess both medicinal and magical values which may or not bear a relationship to each other. A Witch might prescribe vervain medicinally to cure a headache or to be used as a diuretic, eyewash or throat gargle. On the magical level, however, she or he might recommend it as a love talisman or in a spell to overcome fear.

Herbal Talismans

Plants can be combined in "mojo bags" (small red flannel bags) and carried to ward off disease and other negative influences or to attract positive, healthy vibrations. One of my favorite types of herbal talismans and one of the simplest to make is a planetary sachet. It uses powdered herbs and a few drops of an appropriate perfume oil and fixative to preserve the herbs' potency and aroma.

Influences of the Sun and Mercury are most commonly invoked for good health. The Sun acts magically on the right eye, pituitary and thyroid glands, heart, spleen and spine. It is also good for spiritual cleansing and to build self-confidence. The Sun's plants include acacia, aloes, almond, angelica, ash, bay laurel, burnet, celadine, centaury, chamomile, chicory, clove, corn, dandelion, datura, eyebright, heart trefoil, juniper, lignum vitae, lovage, meadow rue, mistletoe, orange tree, pineapple, rice, rosemary, rue, salvia, St. John's wort, spearmint and walnut.

The healing action of Mercury is applied to the brain, mouth, nervous system, pituitary, thyroid and parathyroid glands, pulmonary and respiratory circulation and vocal chords. The plants associated with Mercury include anise, Brazil nut, calamint, caraway, carrot, cashew, cinnamon, cinquefoil, citron, dill, elecampagne, fennel, fenugreek, filbert, hazel, houndstongue, horehound, lavender, licorice, linseed, maidenhair, marjoram, mulberry, oat, orris, parsley, parsnip, peyote, pennyroyal, savory, southernwood, valerian and wintergreen.

When preparing a herbal talisman, use any of these plants, which usually are available at health-food stores or from mail-order herb suppliers. Some of the more common herbs can be found in grocery stores or if you are more ambitious, you may grow, harvest and dry your own. I like to use six herbs for Sun talismans and eight for Mercury because these are the numerical equivalents of these planets according to the doctrine of signatures.

Consecration of Talismans

To activate the herbs' psychic potencies, perform the following rite of consecration for a Sun herbal talisman on a Sunday. You will want to gather ahead of time as many solar symbols as possible for two reasons: to stimulate your imagination and to draw the planet's strength. (In astrological terms, the Sun is a "planet.") The more correspondences you can muster, the more potent the talisman.

Obtain the following: two yellow candles, a yellow silk cloth for the altar (if possible, embroider or paint it with a Sun symbol), cinnamon oil to anoint the candles, heliotrope oil to anoint the talisman, marigold flowers for the altar, frankincense and myrrh incense (to burn on quick-lighting charcoal in an incense burner), two two-inch squares of yellow cotton or silk cut into the shape of a hexagon, an ounce or two of six different powdered "solar" herbs, a needle and yellow thread, scissors and two small bowls, one containing salt, symbolizing Earth, and one of water.

Arrange the items on the altar as in the diagram.

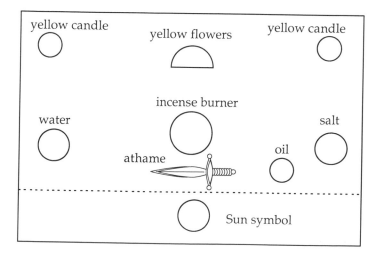

Light the candles and incense and open a circle. Some Witches use a traditional Wicca circle opening, which involves purifying the circle with symbols of the four elements. Others choose to purify, consecrate and invoke by intoning the ceremonial magicians' Pentagram Ritual. Others might use methods from African Voodoo or Native American practice. Choose the way with which you are most comfortable or follow suggestions given in "Seasonal Rites / Magical Rites" for opening a circle.

After opening the circle, face south to call upon the Sun god Apollo. Say something like:

> Great god Apollo, you who are perfection in form, golden healer, I call upon you to descend into this circle of light. Surround me with your liquid fire. Protect me from negativity and imbalance with your righteous rays and guide me toward the astral light.

After a moment's contemplation, add six drops of heliotrope oil to the herbs on the altar and mix well. Spread one of the pieces of yellow cloth on the altar and drop the herbal mixture on it. Cover with the other cloth and sew shut.

Add more incense to the burner if needed, and then pass the talisman bag through the smoke. Say, "Talisman for health, by virtue of the power of Apollo the mighty Sun god, I consecrate you with air."

Quickly pass the talisman through the candle flame and repeat the above phrase substituting "fire" for "air." Similarly, consecrate with water by sprinkling water on the talisman with your fingers and substituting "water" in the phrase, then with earth by sprinkling on a pinch of salt and substituting "earth."

Now hold the talisman in the palm of your left hand

and with the first and second fingers of your right hand or your athame (ritual dagger) if you have one, recite:

> *By the virtues of the power of Sun, life-giving orb that brightens and warms our days, I hereby consecrate this talisman. May it ever work to improve* (the patient's name) *health so she (he) may soon be well and walk in the sunshine. So mote it be!*

(You may wish to reverse hands if you are left-handed.)

Thank any unseen entities that may have been attracted to your ritual and reverently end it, snuffing the candles and pouring leftover salt, water and ash onto the ground. The talisman is ready to present to the patient to carry in purse or pocket or pin on clothing.

Perform the Mercury talisman consecration rite on a Wednesday in the same general way. Use the following correspondences: orange candles, violet altar cloth, multicolored talisman cloth cut into octagons, orange thread, lilac oil for the candles, narcissus oil for the herbs, cinnamon and sandalwood incense, and lavender flowers for the altar. Invoke the god-form Hermes while facing east. Compose a personal prayer to the god.

Here is an example from our coven annals of how to use an herbal talisman. The toddler son of one coven member suffered from a persistent skin rash that defied both homeopathic and traditional medical care.

During a waning Moon in Aries, we acquired something that belonged to him—a piece cut from a cloth diaper—and a teaspoon each of crushed basil leaves, yarrow flowers, comfrey leaves and four balm-of-Gilead buds. I molded a green clay figure to represent the child (green for Libra, his birth sign). We laid down a small square of bluish-purple cloth (the color at the opposite end of the spectrum from red, which represents skin eruptions) and on top of it placed the diaper piece, clay figure and herbs.

We performed a consecration ritual and directed energy into the ingredients, anointing the clay figure with rose oil to which we added a few drops of lavender oil. Afterwards we tied up the bag with a piece of blue yarn and took the consecrated herbal talisman to the baby's mother to hang over his crib. Within three days the rash disappeared.

Circle Healing

When the patient can be present, an effective psychic healing technique is a group circle healing rite. This ritual requires no special equipment except the concentrated visualized force of will of each covener. The high priestess or priest opens the circle in the coven's customary manner, and the coveners sit in a circle facing in and holding hands. The patient sits alone in the center.

The group begins to chant something like "shen-ur" (circle of life—Egyptian), "Raphael," (archangel of healing—Hebrew) or "corpus sans" (healthy body—Latin), at the same time visualizing a current of bluish-white electric light descend from the cosmos, enter each person's head and travel down the left shoulder, arm and out the left hand. The light passes into the next covener's right hand and moves across the body until it links with the light streaming into that person's body from above. The ray of light then flows out through the left hand, passing onto the next covener, and so on until the circle is connected by a scintillating band of bluish-white light. As this happens, everyone's hands should begin to tingle with power.

While energy builds, the coveners visualize that the

light rises slowly from their circle and reforms as a cone suspended over the patient's head. Still chanting, the coveners will the cone to descend until it completely encases the patient.

At this point, the chanting grows progressively stronger and faster as the coveners respond to the energy flow. It is difficult to describe how or when the chanting stops as this needs to be experienced to be understood. It intensifies until it peaks, and intuitively everyone stops chanting at once and releases hands.

Then begins the two-part healing segment. First, the healers direct the "light" still flowing from their vibrating hands into the patient in order to absorb the negativity produced by the illness. Sometimes one can feel the negativity enter the hands like a heavy, cold, or hot lump and rise up as far as the elbows. When this happens, the healer immediately shakes out the hands to remove the negativity, aiming them to the outside of the circle behind the group and away from the patient. (If absorbed negativity is not expelled, the healer may fall ill.) This procedure is repeated three to nine times.

Next the coveners extend their hands toward the patient again, but this time they will the "light" to penetrate the patient's body and fill it with healing energy. To keep the energy flowing and the hands vibrating it is helpful to rub them together occasionally. Repeat this procedure, rubbing hands together, three to nine times until all the energy has been depleted and the cone of power and ring of bluish-white light have dissolved.

It is important to expend all the energy produced by the coven in the healing. Excess energy remaining in the body is often too powerful for it and if left to accumulate can damage the healer's own body.

Not every healing attempt succeeds. I remember one resounding failure that bears telling for the lesson it shows. A few years ago we gathered together a large group for Hallowmas festivities. Excitement and expectation permeated the atmosphere as usual before an important celebration.

We decided to take advantage of the high energy generated by our rite and perform a healing on one of our initiates, Sabrina, who recently had suffered a broken nose in a car accident. We placed her in the center of the circle and worked a healing rite as outlined above.

At the ritual's conclusion, one of my Craft students came up to me with her face aglow. She had recently undergone catastrophic changes in her life, and I was happy to see her in a better mood. She gushed about how wonderful the ritual was and that the part she enjoyed most was the healing. She could hardly wait to do another.

With all the merrymaking that night I never had a chance to talk to Sabrina. When I inquired a few days later how she felt, she quickly asked, "Who was sitting two people away from you during the healing? When you all directed the light toward me I began to feel an incredible energy surround my body. Suddenly I felt it all drawn off in that direction like through a siphon. What a disappointment!"

Needless to say, the drain was from the student. No doubt unconsciously her acute need for energy drove her to take it away from the intended recipient. I should never have allowed her to participate in the healing segment of the ritual.

So I urge you to learn from my mistake and never attempt to perform a healing unless you are in the proper frame of mind and adequately prepared for the task.

Regardless of the method used, healing can be an exhilaratingly satisfying activity that creates a purpose for and reaffirms one's faith in Witchcraft. Still, always bear in mind that the power generated by healing, whether in a group, with magical herbs, chromotherapy or any other method, is not the healer's personal power. The Witch is the conductor or transmitter of cosmic energy from "above" to "below." Nothing sets the Witch apart from other people just because he or she is trained to attract and direct this power. Thinking otherwise will eventually dissipate the magical force and drain the Witch's personal energy. Thank the Lady and the Lord for that which is not yours but has flowed through you on its way to those in need. To give freely to others is the greatest healing tonic of all and possibly the key to the secret of the elixir of life.

ABOUT THE AUTHOR

Morwyn has studied Witchcraft for more than twenty years, having been initiated by Lady Sara Cunningham. She is priestess of the Coven of Trer Drwy and owner of an aromatherapy business. She is the author of *Secrets of a Witch's Coven* and of a forthcoming book on Brazilian magic, *Pomba-Gira: Enchantments of the Female Messenger of the Gods*. Two other books, *Web of Light* and *Witch's Brew* are awaiting publication at this time. Morwyn lives in Boulder, Colorado, with her family and 22-year-old cat and, in addition to writing, works as a cross-cultural trainer. She enjoys jogging, gardening, traveling and remodeling her historic home.

NOTES

[1] This viewpoint is discussed in Mary Chamberlain, *Old Wives' Tales: Their History, Remedies and Spells*, London: Virago Press, 1981.

[2] For a more precise definition and historical discussion, see Lewis Spence, *An Encyclopedia of Occultism*, Secaucus, New Jersey: The Citadel Press, 1960, 1977.

[3] These and other fascinating details about the influence of light and color on our lives are presented in the hallmark study by Faber Birren, *Color Psychology and Color Therapy*, Secaucus, New Jersey: The Citadel Press, 1950, 1961.

Sex Magic

by Valerie Voigt

Western Pagan religions differ from monotheistic religions in several ways: we take responsibility for our own actions rather than blaming our mistakes on imaginary devils; we find the sacred in the here and now rather than in some remote Big Daddy in the Sky and distant heaven; and we worship Nature. Pagan religions have traditionally seen sex as an integral part of this Nature-reverence. As an expression of holiness, sacramental sex was practiced in the temples in Sumer, the first civilization in the Western World. The king and the high priestess of the city were joined in an annual ceremony of sacred marriage, magic to ensure the welfare of the land. Embodying the Goddess Inanna and the God Dumuzi, the high priestess and the king thus blessed the fields and herds with abundant fertility, and the people thereby with wealth and well-being.

Indeed, since all civilization is based on agricultural surplus, we have those early peoples, their high priestesses and kings, to thank for our very existence!

The annual Sacred Marriage was not the only sex magic performed in Sumer. Nor was heterosexual magic the only sort. Indeed, throughout the Eastern Mediterranean, and in many other parts of the ancient world, people of all walks of life performed private ceremonies or went to the great temples of Astarte, Artemis, Aphrodite, Hathor, and other Goddesses to receive blessings and healing from the Goddess. Down to the present day, this sacred practice has survived to bring joy, balance, and health to those who follow the Old Ways. This ritual, the Great Rite, is one of the most important ceremonies in the Craft.

How Sex Magic Works

When you have loving, communicative, responsible sex, you are automatically balancing your energy. The energy that has been floating sluggishly or randomly in your body and aura focuses, flows, and clarifies. If you are having that sex with a partner, you balance not only your individual energies, but also the flow of energy between the two of you.

Witches know that the Universe is a living entity, a dance and union of sacred forces in a great wheel of life. We are part of that dance; indeed, we participate in its creation. When we make love, we can be especially aware of our place in the Creative Force because we are focusing our divine energy. We can actively and consciously connect with God, with Goddess, and experience that creation.

Sex magic starts with polarity, the attraction which exists when energy can flow readily between two points: between people, or between one part of you and another part, or between you and any other part of the Universe, or even between you and the Universe as a whole. In the imagery of bodily fertility, these creative forces are Goddess and God, Whom partners can embody. Yet the so-called "fertility religions," including the Craft, have never been limited to the heterosexual roles of physical fertility. The ancient temples were home to sacred ecstasy of every kind, because our ancestors always knew that love of every kind is creative on the spiritual and personal level. Even today, the Charge of the Goddess says, in part, "All acts of love and pleasure are My rituals."

Sex also raises power: power which may be enjoyed for its own sake or directed in thaumaturgy (magic-working). I have been in several covens, and the most powerful magic was performed by those in which there was some flow of sexual electricity among the members, even though in the majority of these there was no actual sexual activity.

Most Witches prefer to do most sex magic within the context of consecrated magical partnerships. A partnership may be a permanent life partnership (such as a marriage), a committed but strictly ceremonial partnership or a temporary partnership formed for a specific purpose or period of time. In most successful partnerships the partners are deeply in love. In all cases, however, some attraction or "chemistry" between the partners is needed for the magic to be effective; real partnerships cannot be formed at random, or against the true feelings of any partner.

Partnerships are often formalized with a handfasting or consecration ritual. A handfasting is a Wiccan magical marriage, and may have all the bonding and permanence of any marriage, or may last for a set period of time. Traditionally, a year and a day used to be a common duration, but partners are free to choose the time for themselves, or to formalize the duration for "as long as love shall last." Many, perhaps most, Witches consecrate their partnerships as permanent. We often obtain marriage licenses and register our handfastings as legal marriages.

In no case can a valid magical partnership exist when one partner is manipulating another or bringing pressure to bear, no matter how subtle or unconscious that pressure may be. When people hold unequal power (such as a teacher and student, a landlord and tenant, a supervisor and an employee), it is very difficult—in most cases impossible—for the relationship to be free enough to allow a magical partnership.

In my years as a high priestess I have occasionally heard of self-proclaimed "teachers" or "high priest/esse/s" who required their students to warm their beds. Such people defile the sacredness of divine energy, and the karmic price they (and their students) pay is heavy. Sometimes their students stay on, believing that they must pay this price in order to learn, but such "teachers" have so little understanding of themselves, let alone the Universe, that they usually have little if anything useful to teach.

Although it is a blessing to have a good teacher in the Craft, it is never right to go against your own feelings or sense of privacy. Nowadays, there are many excellent books available so that you can learn the Craft on your own. Even if there were no books, the Goddess is fully capable of teaching Her own without books! What She requires is a clear heart, an open mind, self-honesty, courage, and a willingness to work hard.

Getting Started

In this chapter I am not discussing Eastern Tantra or other esoteric disciplines. My purpose is to provide information and exercises that will allow anyone whose heart wills it to begin learning practical Western sex magic. Of course, you can also learn much, from teachers or books, about kundalini yoga, Tantra, and the sacred mythology of sex and fertility deities, and I encourage you to do so. Books about sexuality itself are also good.

In the exercises and rituals that follow, some details are not specified. This is not because of prudery or secrecy, but because sex magic must involve pleasure. Where details are unspecified, you should choose what is pleasurable to you (and to your partner, if any), within the structure of the ceremony. This chapter is not a list of recipes, but rather a template for you to adapt and expand for your own needs.

Health and good hygiene are especially important for a sex magician. Keep your body clean; eat a nutritious diet, and minimize the junk food. You may find it easier to do energy work if you are following a protein-balanced vegetarian diet. And of course, use contraception in any situation when sex could result in unwanted pregnancy!

Safe sex is perfectly effective for sex magic. Furthermore, activity which compromises your health and safety or that of your partner is likely to hurt your magic. Bear this in mind when you plan and prepare your workings.

Energy work takes practice even if you have a natural talent for it. If you have trouble getting any part of any magical exercise to happen, close your eyes so that your conscious vision will not interfere with your inner vision. If you still do not sense it, visualize it anyway: visualization helps prepare the pathways and begins the movement of energy, so repeated practice will help you accomplish the full exercise. Of course, you should feel free to improvise appropriate words if you are feeling creative.

Some teachers would feel that parts of the following exercises are too advanced for beginners, and that I am rushing you. I can state from my personal experience, however, that many beginners are able to accomplish the complete exercises right away, because various life experiences have prepared them already. Others may need to practice for some time before achieving proficiency. Do not feel discouraged if it takes you a while.

Sex Magic for One—Basic Exercise

Solitary sex magic is the best starting point. Learning about your own body and energy is good preparation for other work, and is useful in itself. This exercise is designed to start you in several different aspects of sex magic. It helps you learn to feel and nourish your own energy. It gets you in touch with your unmixed energy. It also helps you tune in to divine forces, and with sufficient focus can be transformative as well. It is a good idea to do this one several times a year, to balance your development.

Choose a time when you can have at least two hours to yourself. As you would for any ceremony, take a ritual bath in warm water. Optionally, add a few drops of oil, or add herbs (see below for information about these). Light a white candle. Clear your mind and relax.

When you are ready, dry off and cast your circle in your usual way. Light a green candle and anoint yourself with sandalwood oil. Feel your body; caress it lovingly and feel its power. In a comfortable position, focus your awareness on your spinal cord and draw a column of white spirit-fire up from the base of your spine to the top of your skull. As the fire rises, it may shoot flames out through your limbs; this is good, so encourage it.

For Women

In the Time Before Time, the Star Goddess gave birth to the Universe and to all the other deities. With the sacred fire burning within you, invoke the Star Goddess Whose body encircles the Universe:

> *O Great Mother, Queen of Heaven, I am Thy daughter. I am Thy fire. I am Thyself. Be with me and in me as I give birth to the Universe.*

As you personify the Star Goddess, feel in your belly the swelling and contraction of birth. Encircle your vulva with your hands; touch your body in pleasure and build the power in your body. When you feel the power fully, take a deep breath and blow, pressing down with your diaphragm as you do so. As you press down, feel the great ball of energy born from your womb, and see it take form as stars, planets, and shining creatures.

Raise your arms and feel your body shining. Speak:

> *My children, Blessed Be!*

Place your hands upon your heart, drawing the energy contained in the Circle and focusing it there:

> *Blessed I am.*

Drink from the chalice and rest. You have just released quite a bit of energy into the circle, and blessed yourself with it. When ready, dismiss the quarters and open the circle.

For Men

In the Great Beginning, the God Khepera pleasured himself and masturbated the other Gods into existence. With the sacred fire burning within you, invoke Khepera:

O Great Father, Lord of Power, I am Thy son. I am Thy fire. I am Thyself. Be with me and in me as I bring forth the Universe.

As you personify Khepera, take your phallus in both hands and speak:

Sacred staff of power, source of life and joy, with thee I bless the world.

Pleasure yourself, building the power with your physical excitement. Imagine the power as a growing spirit-flame, which fills your body but is hottest at the base of your phallus. As you approach orgasm, feel the great fire focus. With your orgasm, the spirit-fire shoots outward with your semen as stars, planets, and shining creatures, and flows outward from your heart as love. The shining creatures take form as Gods, Goddesses, and living creatures of the Earth.

Raise your arms and feel your body shining. Speak:

My children, Blessed Be!

Place your hands upon your heart, drawing the energy contained in the Circle and focusing it there:

I am.

Drink from the chalice and rest. You have just released quite a bit of energy into the circle and blessed yourself with it. When ready, dismiss the quarters and open the circle.

After you have done this basic exercise, you may adapt it for tuning in to other gods and goddesses. As you become more advanced, you should experiment with the version of this exercise for the other gender. You may also introduce symbolic elemental alchemy as a new dimension to the exercise.

Sex Magic for Two—Basic Exercise

In Woody Allen's film *Bananas*, Allen has just made love to the leading lady. She gasps, "That was like a religious experience—how do you do it?" Allen replies with a shrug, "Well, I practice a lot when I'm alone."

I hope you do the same, because the magic you do with partners will be better if you practice alone as well. I hope also that you work actively to overcome any shyness and communicate with your partner. Most problems that arise in sex magic are actually relationship problems, and most relationship problems are communication problems.

In sex magic for two you celebrate and share your sacred energy with a partner, radiating power and amplifying it together. You may begin with this exercise, which you should read through completely before carrying out. This is both a celebratory and a transformative exercise; later you can use it in theurgy (union with divine forces) and thaumaturgy as well.

Prepare the circle in your usual way. Light a white candle in the center of your altar. With oil of amber, anoint each other as follows:

Blessed Be thy feet.
Blessed Be thy knees.
Blessed Be thy vulva/phallus.
Blessed Be thy breasts.
Blessed Be thy lips.
Blessed Be thy Third Eye.
Blessed Be thy Vision Point.

(The Third Eye is in the middle of the forehead; the Vision Point is the large vertebra at the base of the neck.)

Anoint also a red candle, and hold it between your bodies:

Candle red as blood, blood red as fire, fire in our
blood, bright our desire.

Light the candle and place it on the altar.

As you proceed, tune in to your partner's soul and feelings. As you gain practice with this exercise, you will be able to sense your partner's body in new ways which will enhance your workings and inspire you to improvise.

Face each other. Speak in turn:

Sacred one, My beloved, Thou art the flesh Of
the Holy One. Thou art God/dess. I honor You and
to Your holiness I offer my own.

Keeping ever mindful of your holiness, kiss and proceed.

The first part of this exercise is called the Pentacle of Kisses.

Your partner lies in the pentacle position (arms outstretched, feet apart). You gently begin kissing, starting with the top of the foot and moving slowly up the body. With each kiss, move bright spirit-fire energy up from your genital area through your body to your lips, so that each kiss is made with a burst of spirit-fire. (You may find that the spirit-fire leaves trails of sparkling sensation in your body; if so, it's good, as it helps build the energy.) When you reach your partner's diaphragm area (about five inches below the heart), add to your kiss there a deep warm breath, gently blowing the spirit-fire blessing into your partner's body. Continue kissing until you reach your partner's heart. Blow another spirit-fire blessing into your partner's heart, then listen to the heartbeat for a minute.

Start over with the top of your partner's other foot, and repeat. Repeat again with the top of each hand and the top of the head. As arousal increases, and as the spirit-fire glows brighter, energy rises out of the Earth, filling the circle.

Trade places with your partner.

As your partner begins to kiss you, tune in very closely. Be very aware of your body. Feel the spirit-fire of each kiss, and feel the tingling traces left by each. When your partner blows the spirit-fire into your heart, feel your heart open to its warmth.

When you have finished both Pentacles of Kisses, lie together heart to heart, hip to hip. Feel the Earth-power around you. Feel the spirit-fire traces on your skins, mirroring each other, and sense the spirit-fire that now fills your bodies. Greet each other:

Blessed Be, Holy One.

As you make love, let the spirit-fire grow until it glows out into your auras and merges, so that the two of you are engulfed in a single flame of which your bodies are the twin sources. Remain tuned in to each other's spirits as much as to your bodies (lying temple-to-temple usually helps, but don't let that short-circuit your spontaneity). The more tuned in you are to each other, the more harmonious your energies and pleasure peaks will be.

If you reach orgasm simultaneously, the spirit-fire will explode in a shower of sparks, and you will probably feel the sparks all over you. You may be completely breathless, or even paralyzed. Don't worry; medical emergencies are unlikely. It is almost unheard of to die this way. (But when I must go, this will be my preferred method!)

If you do not reach orgasm simultaneously, not to worry. Simply continue until the second partner has peaked.

Place your hands upon each other's hearts, drawing the energy contained in the Circle and focusing it there:

Blessed Be.

Drink from the chalice and rest. When ready, dismiss the quarters and open the circle.

When you are proficient with this exercise, you may experience a sensation of having switched bodies with your partner. You may experience a temporary loss of ego or of boundaries; you may spontaneously spirit-project or leave your body. These are wonderful mystical experiences, and I believe they cannot be forced; but they can be scary if they come as a complete surprise. If they happen, don't be frightened; just relax and enjoy (or do magical work in these states; once they happen, you'll know what to do). If you've already had these experiences, the odds are you don't need this chapter! Once you have some experience with these exercises, you can do magical work with them. You can consecrate or charge tools and talismans by placing them on, between, or beneath you. You can raise energy to focus and send toward a desired goal. You can attune yourself to specific deities while you perform the exercises by invoking them into the circle or into each other. Do the latter only with proper purification and preparation and be sure to set up the circle properly. Once the invocations are done, be fully aware that you are acting as deities and conduct yourself in a fitting manner.

Male-female couples may choose to attune to Inanna and Dumuzi, or Medb and Ailill, or Frigga and Odin. Male-male couples, likewise, might choose Shiva and Agni, or Apollo and Dionysos, while female-female couples might choose Artemis and Her various nymphs. Anyone exploring gender issues might do well to study, and perhaps do solitary or group attunement rituals, to Dionysos, Hermaphroditos, Cybele, Inanna, Ishtar, and other Deities whose ancient myths or rituals included a blurring of gender distinctions. Many deities, for example Dionysos or Cybele, have been worshiped orgiastically as well. If you are not sure which deities you wish to work with, you may (as most Witches probably do) wait for them to come to you, but trips to your library's mythology and history sections may also prove instructive.

Once partners are well-established as a working couple, they may choose to do occasional rituals in which, rather than raising energy in both partners equally, one partner is taken to a physically ecstatic state by the other, who remains in a sensitive but methodical state of mind. This technique of achieving a mystical state by overloading the sensory circuits allows the ecstatic partner to gain self-knowledge, knowledge of the cosmos, visions, and occasionally the second sight.

Sex Magic for More Than Two

In general, the exercises and rituals described above apply to groups as well as to solitaries and couples. Sex magic for more than two is usually more complicated, however, primarily because it is difficult to focus attention and energy effectively on more than one person. Here are some workable solutions.

Focusing all the energy through one central person at a time often works well. One person is in the middle, and the others channel their energy to or through that person either through making love to him/her simultaneously or by moving their energy through another intermediate partner to the central person. The latter works well if the group is mixed in sexual orientation; in such cases, bisexuals usually mediate the energy among the others.

Another solution is to focus as if the group were an electrical circuit, that is, to concentrate on the energy itself, rather than on any individual member of the group. The energy moves from one person to the next and the next, deosil around a circle. Superficially, the effect may seem impersonal because group members may, for the duration of the ritual, submerge their personalities into their functions as energy channels. This is most likely to occur in gender-balanced heterosexual groups and single-gender homosexual groups, but can work well in other groups as well.

A third solution is to move the sexual energy abstractly rather than physically. This can work well if the group's orientation mixture is inconvenient, since energy is focused on an object or goal, with energy amplified among the many complex abstract psychic circuits rather than through bodily ones.

This third method is surprisingly common and can

work well for anyone: individual, pair, or group of any size. The idea of sex magic without any overt sexual activity may seem odd at first but is a natural corollary of the Pagan view that sex is both a process and an energy rather than a narrow set of actions.

Tips and Techniques

Men tend to be quicker to arouse than women. This means that mixed-gender couples usually need to take extra time to tune into each other, since their rhythms are different. Single-gender couples tune in to each other's rhythms more easily, but male couples should still take extra time, so that the depth of the power can build.

The clitoris contains as many nerves as the penis, but these nerves are concentrated in a much smaller spot which needs gentle treatment.

Orthodox scientific research indicates that about one man in six has erotically sensitive nipples. Judging from my personal experience, I would say that about four more of the six do too but have not had their erotic power awakened to that extent. Patience and gentleness have coaxed into bloom the erogenous nipples of many a man who stated firmly, "My nipples aren't sensitive at all."

The much-vaunted "G-Spot" is named after the man who thinks he was the first to discover it (sigh). With the help of a wonderful lover, I, like most of the other Pagan women I know, learned about the "magic spot" long before "Dr. G." ever did his research. In most women, it's about four to five inches inside the vagina—rather deep. The magic spot, like the clitoris, should never be treated roughly, so if you touch it with your fingers be careful. If you touch it with a phallus, you needn't be so careful if the woman is fully aroused. Steady, rhythmic, smooth strokes seem to work best for most women.

Men too have a magic spot: the prostate gland, located inside, above and behind the testicles. It is extremely sensitive and often responds best to steady, rhythmic, smooth touch. You may press gently but firmly behind the testicles to find it; it does not feel obvious, but it is there, as the man being touched can tell you, especially after a couple of minutes. If the man is lying on his back, a well-lubricated finger moving gradually into his anus and pressed gently toward his penis will caress the prostate. If the man is not too shy, this usually gives him much pleasure. In such cases, fingernails should be clipped extremely short and filed smooth, and rubber gloves should be used, since a condom will not fit over a whole hand. External moderately firm caressing of the prostate can prolong and intensify orgasm dramatically for some men; so can internal touch, but generous amounts of lubricant are needed. Use a water-based liquid or gel lubricant; spit is only a last resort in this case.

It is relatively seldom that men experience the sort of rhythmic, sweeping, full-body, cosmic orgasm that so many women do. As a general rule, the men who do experience it are receiving attention to their prostates at the time.

A woman or man can guide a male lover to the magic spot by lying on his or her back, a pillow beneath the hips, and slipping the partner's phallus deeply inside. If the top partner is still, the bottom partner can do the moving, and "ride" him. If the partners are fully aroused, the magic spot will probably be easy to find. In anal intercourse, this may also be fairly easy if the bottom partner is on his or her stomach (again, partners should be fully aroused and well-lubricated first; some experimentation with angle may be necessary).

If the top partner is female, or if both partners are female, they can use these same procedures although with some improvisation.

Lying temple-to-temple, with or without sex, can help you and your partner attune to each other.

Condoms are available in many colors and can be chosen by color to harmonize with the working.

When people are fully aroused, their physical sensory processes change. Sensations which would normally be perceived as tickling (or even mild pain) may turn pleasurable instead. Psychologists call this "re-attribution of arousal." Should you choose to use re-attribution of arousal for much beyond gentle biting, you really should have special training. If you cannot get such training, please do not risk your or your partner's safety; be very careful of delicate areas (including the kidney area, the abdomen, the anus, and the face). "Scourging to gain the Sight" has been mentioned in many books, and so must be mentioned here: the scourge's thongs should be short and plain (they can be made of silk), and the wielder knowledgeable about anatomy. For safety, scourging must be restricted to the back, shoulders, and buttocks only.

Many people seem to have an unconscious need to unite with primal Sacred Powers by surrendering to them. I think this is why many women—and men, too— have a ravishment fantasy (not a rape fantasy). This is also one reason why many people have used some form of bondage to achieve an ecstatic state: the surrender allows the person to give up all the control normally held by the linear mind—control which may have become so habitual as to interfere with voluntary changes of consciousness.

Avoiding Common Pitfalls

Not all deities of sex or love are properly worshiped with sexual rites. The Yoruba Goddess Oshun, for example, likes sex but does not want it to be performed in the room with Her shrine.

Do not use sex magic for all your rituals. For some (necromancy, for example) it is not only highly inappropriate but also potentially dangerous. Give serious thought when planning any ritual.

Do not assume anyone you are attracted to would be a good partner in sex magic or would want to participate. Sexual mysticism is a common underlying trait of most Western Paganism; but sex magic is, by and large, a magical specialty rather than a topic of general interest.

Likewise, do not use magic as an excuse for sex. You do not need an excuse for sex. If you need an excuse, you are suffering from leftover patriarchal and/or Judeo-Christian prudery. Prudery is bondage, and Pagans are a free people; banish prudery from your life. Have sex when you (and your partners) agree that you wish to, as long as you harm none thereby.

Do not use sex magic, or any other form of magic, carelessly. Respect the awesome power of the sacred forces you move with your magic.

Resources

I recommend that you have a "Great Rite Kit" with clean towels, lubricants, special oils, and other supplies all in one place. Keep it well supplied and handy. Suggested basic contents:

- condoms
- contraceptives
- ritual oils

- massage oils
- lubricants (the water-based type are usually preferable)
- toys, if appropriate
- towels
- laundry bag

Suppliers

There are many suppliers of lubricants, oils, and other supplies for sex. These two have both been in business for many years at their current addresses, and have built excellent reputations with their high quality products:

Eve's Garden, 119 West 57th St., Ste. 420, New York, New York 10019; (212) 757-8651 or (800) 848-3837—$2 for catalog.

Good Vibrations, 1210 Valencia Street, San Francisco, California 94110; (415) 550-7399 (mail order); (415) 550-0827 (retail store)—$3 for both book catalog and toy and supply catalog.

Information

San Francisco Sex Information Hotline: (415) 621-7300
Los Angeles Sex Information Helpline: (213) 653-1123
AIDS Foundation Hotline: (800) FOR-AIDS

Herbs, Incenses, and Oils for Sex Magic

To save space, this list is restricted to scents and herbs specific to sex magic. If you wish to add herbs, incenses, and oils associated with the various practical goals (healing, etc.) consult any of the excellent herbals and handbooks available.

Purpose	Incenses	Oils	Herbs*
General	frankincense, sandalwood	frankincense, sandalwood	mugwort, peppermint
Invocatory of most sex Goddesses in Western traditions	musk, amber, jasmine	musk, amber	lemon balm, mints (peppermint, spearmint, etc.), rose, lavender, orris root
Invocatory of most sex Gods in Western traditions	musk, amber, civet, patchouli	musk, amber civet, patchouli	patchouli, blessed thistle, southernwood
Invocatory of Inanna, Ishtar, Dumuzi, and other Middle Eastern deities	cinnamon, frankincense, myrrh (use myrrh with care, as it is also sacred to Hecate and other Dark Goddesses)	cinnamon, frankincense, myrrh	cinnamon, frankincense, myrrh, cedar,
Romance	rose, lavender, mint, jasmine	rose, lavender, pennyroyal (do not use pennyroyal oil if the ritual involves a pregnant woman)	parsley, sage, rosemary, thyme, rowan, mistletoe, orris root, damiana
Fertility	sandalwood, mistletoe, cedar, cinnamon, mace	sandalwood, cinnamon, jasmine	basil, nutmeg, broom, catnip, mandrake, oak, acorn, mistletoe
Mystical Union	sandalwood, musk, amber, lavender, dragon's blood	sandalwood, musk, amber, lavender	mugwort, wormwood, blue vervain, coriander, broom

Purpose	Incenses	Oils	Herbs*
Transformation	sandalwood, musk, lemon, dragon's blood	sandalwood, musk, patchouli	mugwort, wormwood, coriander, summer savory, mandrake
Ecstasy	amber, musk, sandalwood, jasmine	amber, musk sandalwood	amber, blessed thistle, rosemary, tormantil
Attracting a Lover	musk, amber, cinnamon, lemon, myrrh	musk, amber, myrrh	cinnamon, lemon peel, mandrake, orris root, rosemary, meadowsweet
Marriage	musk, amber, rose, camphor,	olive, musk, amber, rose	rose, orange peel, orange blossoms, orris root

*For bath infusions, sprinkling, scattering, or use in talismans. Some of these herbs are poisonous, so do not consume unless you know which are which!

I hope that this brief introduction to sex magic is useful to you. Work hard, play hard, and Blessed Be!

ABOUT THE AUTHOR

Valerie Voigt has practiced as a Priestess of Ishtar and Dionysos since the early 1970s. She received certification in sex information counseling in 1984. She has worked counseling clients at Sensual Magic in San Francisco, and has also worked as a hotline counselor at San Francisco Sex Information, a nonprofit public education organization. She has reviewed sex education materials for local churches and community organizations. She has also studied Kundalini Yoga. Her training and practice in several traditions of Wicca and her degree work in classical languages have contributed to her study of sex magic as a specialty, but she is quick to state that her teachings about sex magic are not based on any single tradition of the Craft. She co-founded the Centre of the Divine Ishtar in 1982, and continues to work with Centre members in rituals designed to heal the Earth and promote and celebrate its fertility.

SUGGESTIONS FOR FURTHER READING

Books Primarily About Sex

Some of these books are available in public libraries, but others are not. Most of them are available from the two suppliers listed above. Most of these books were written before the emergence of the AIDS epidemic. Be sure to educate yourself thoroughly about AIDS and other sexually transmissible diseases before participating in sex magic with a partner.

Blank, Joani. *Playbook for Men about Sex.* Burlingame, California: Down There Press, 1976.

_____. *Playbook for Women about Sex.* Burlingame, California: Down There Press, 1976.

Califia, Pat. *Sapphistry,* 3rd revised edition. New York: Pergamon, 1988.

Comfort, Alex, ed. *The Joy of Sex.* New York: Simon and Schuster, 1972.

Delaney, Martin, and Goldblum, Peter. *Strategies for Survival: A Gay Men's Health Manual for the Age of AIDS.* New York: St. Martin's Press, 1987.

Preston, John, and Swann, Glenn. *Safe Sex: The Ultimate Erotic Guide.* New York: New American Library, 1987.

Raley, Patricia. *Making Love: How to Be Your Own Sex Therapist.* New York: Dial Press, 1976.

Walker, Mitch. *Men Loving Men.* San Francisco: Gay Sunshine Press, 1977.

Magic and Pagan Religion

Bradley, Marion Zimmer. *The Mists of Avalon*. New York: Alfred A. Knopf, Inc., 1982.

Evans, Arthur. *Witchcraft and the Gay Counterculture*. Boston: Fag Rag Books, 1978.

Fortune, Dion. *The Sea Priestess*. New York: Samuel Weiser, Inc. 1978.

Guthrie, W.K.C. *The Greeks and Their Gods*. Boston: Beacon Press, 1950.

Hammond, N.G.L., and Scullard, H.H., eds. *The Oxford Classical Dictionary* (2nd edition). Oxford: Oxford University Press, 1972.

Lewis, I.M. *Ecstatic Religion*. Middlesex, England: Penguin Books, 1971.

Otto, Walter. *Dionysus, Myth and Cult*. Bloomington: Indiana University Press, 1965.

Wolkstein, Diane, and Kramer, Samuel Noah. *Inanna, Queen of Heaven and Earth*. New York: Harper and Row, 1983.

Men and Women in Witchcraft

by Janet & Stewart Farrar

As above, so below. A religion which worships the God and the Goddess as the ultimate creative polarity must envisage—and work with—that same creative polarity of male and female at the human level, otherwise the concepts "God" and "Goddess" are meaningless.

There are, of course, many all-male and even more all-female covens in the Craft with both homosexual and heterosexual orientations. They have their own reasons for their composition, such as wishing to explore Women's Mysteries with gender privacy, and they have every right to follow their own chosen paths. But we think it is fair to say that mainstream Witchcraft consists principally of covens containing both sexes, and that most of these covens regard a numerical balance of women and men as ideal if not always possible. We share this mainstream attitude and will use it as our starting point.

At the divine level, the "male" and "female" polarities may be thought of as coming from a One, an Ultimate which is pure existence, unknowable and untouchable directly (except perhaps in brief flashes of inspiration) until it is polarized, producing the "Supernal Father," raw directionless energy, and the "Supernal Mother," which receives that energy and gives it form.

From this first simple polarization come all manifestations that we call "reality." The Two are the terminals of the Divine Battery, if you like, and the metaphor is an apt one, for if a battery's terminals are not equal and complementary, no current flows.

Of course the cosmic polarization does not remain simple, just raw energy and form giving. It cannot stand still; it must evolve and diversify itself. The male "terminal" produces the qualities of organization and intellect, while the female "terminal" includes the identification and destruction of the outworn and superfluous as well as intuition and emotion.

As it manifests through our planet's most complex species, *Homo/Femina sapiens*, this polarity provides the basis of "male" and "female" distinctions on all levels from physical reproduction to mental and spiritual activity. That is why when a male Witch "draws down the Moon" on his female magical partner, or she "draws down the Sun" on him, their intention is to make her a channel for the Goddess polarity or to make him a channel for the God polarity.

If these principles were not in tune with our essential natures as women and men, the ritual would not work. But everyone who has experienced it sincerely knows that it does.

In our experience, for example, when Stewart "draws down the Moon" on Janet, and then she speaks, sometimes she delivers the traditional Charge of the Goddess without a word altered although often with differing emphasis or tone of delivery appropriate to the occasion. But sometimes her words are completely original, flowing without hesitation and in terms ranging from the movingly poetic to the commandingly emphatic. And these occasions take Janet herself by surprise; she listens to the words and the delivery as though someone else were speaking—as indeed we feel is happening through the channel which we have opened.

What are those male and female "essential natures"? They correspond roughly to what has come to be understood as the left-brain and right-brain functions. To put it at its very simplest, the left half of the brain deals with words and numbers, and the right half with pictures and images. Clinical experience has confirmed this: a person with left-brain damage, for example, has difficulty with reading or calculating while one with right-brain damage finds it hard to recognize even familiar faces.

The strength of the female nature is intuitive and cyclical, emphasizing a situation's totality. It synthesizes, putting things together to see how they relate. The strength of the male nature is intellectual and linear, emphasizing a situation's statistics. It analyzes, taking things to pieces to see what they are made of.

The cyclical and linear aspects can be compared respectively to a spot on a car's tire and the hub of the wheel itself. The first progresses from point A to point B in a series of rhythmic cycles. The hub, meanwhile, covers the same distance at a uniform pace. Yet if the car is working perfectly, both reach their destination at the same time.

You will notice that we say "the strength of" these two natures, not "the whole of." Gender characteristics are a matter of emphasis; they are not exclusive. A whole man, for example, does not lack intuition, nor does a whole woman lack intellect!

The Chinese yin-yang symbol expresses this truth graphically. The white yang (male) half contains a black yin spot, and the black yin (female) half contains a white yang spot. The two are integrated into a balanced whole, but their harmonious polarity could not work if each did not contain an element of the other.

The similar Jungian concept of the anima (the buried feminine element in a man's psyche) and the animus (the buried masculine element in a woman's) relates in most Witches' view to the concept of reincarnation. We believe that the Immortal Self, the reincarnating soul, is composed of male and female elements in perfect balance, but that in any one incarnation one may be either a woman or a man. In that particular incarnation, the feminine or masculine element is emphasized, while the animus or anima represents the complementary element which is (for the duration of that incarnation) secondary.

How does all this apply to a Wiccan male/female working partnership?

Each partner will strive to make the best of what is constructive in his or her male or female emphasis.

The woman will give full expression to her powers of intuition and psychic sensitivity. She will also recognize her cyclical nature: for example, the effect on her psyche of her menstrual and ovulation peaks, which can be very marked.

The man will work to strengthen his conscious awareness, his precise definition of the work at hand. He will strive to extract value from his linear nature as a steadying influence.

But they will do this as a team.

The woman is aware that she must, through their sympathetic resonance, call forth and strengthen the man's psychic awareness to supplement her own. The man is aware that her greater sensitivity also means greater vulnerability and knows he must maintain his linear steadiness to help protect her—and so on.

In spiritual terms, the woman is working to make herself a channel for the Goddess, the feminine aspect at its cosmic best, and the man to make himself a channel for the God in the corresponding way.

In so doing, they are invoking the ultimate Divine polarity as a couple—and also invoking the Divine harmony of that polarity. If they are successful, the Goddess speaks directly through the woman—but she also whispers to the man's anima. And the God speaks directly through the man—but he also whispers to the woman's animus.

Every experienced Wiccan working partnership knows that the pattern we have described is true in general though of course varying in emphasis according to any given couple's component individualities.

We certainly find it true of our own partnership. Stewart is far less psychically sensitive, less giftedly clairvoyant, than Janet, yet this means he is also less vulnerable, less likely to be battered by psychic storms than she is, and so can help to steady and protect her when she does feel battered. Janet, on the other hand, can sense when Stewart's factual analysis is too academic and is missing a situation's overall significance, so she can help him to reassess it.

Janet often tells Stewart that he does not trust his psychic intuition enough, and as a result he has discovered it is more often right than he used to believe. And when Janet is emotionally distressed, and Stewart (as any husband would) tries to comfort her by sharing the distress, she sometimes begs him to "keep your cool," not as indifference, but so that she can draw strength from his detachment.

We sometimes express it (half-jokingly, but with an element of truth) that Janet keeps Stewart's head in the stars while Stewart keeps Janet's feet on the ground.

All this is over-simplified, of course. Janet finds that Stewart's over-tolerant nature sometimes makes him naive and subject to exploitation. Stewart finds that Janet's natural emotions sometimes distort her psychic shrewdness. But then what couple's make-up is ever cut-and-dried? Awareness of complexity strengthens mutual support.

The basic human polarity has been warped by the phases of history.

Until three or four millennia ago, human society was basically matrilinear. The line of descent, and inheritance of property as property developed, was through the mother. This was in accordance with Nature, for we are all born of the mother's womb. In earliest times, the biological nature of paternity was not recognized; women were believed to be impregnated by the Moon's rays or by other means according to various local theories. And even when the facts of impregnation came to be understood, one could only (and of course still can only) be absolutely certain of maternity, not of paternity. This, for example, is why inherited Jewishness is recognized only through the mother, the memories of pogrom rape still being all too recent.

Scholars disagree as to how far early societies were also matriarchal—their public affairs and government conducted by women—but some of them certainly were.

Ancient Egypt was at the transition stage. It was matrilinear but patriarchal. At all levels from pharaoh to peasant, descent and title to property were through the woman, which is why pharaohs so often married their sisters or daughters, to make their claim to the title unchallengeable, and why in dynastic Egypt's last days both Julius Caesar and Anthony made a point of marrying Cleopatra to validate their rule in Egyptian eyes.

For roughly the last two millennia patriarchy has taken over in politics, economics, religion and the psychological attitudes which underlie them all. The masculine aspect, which should be one half of a creative polarity, became distorted to a dictatorship, with the feminine aspect mistrusted and tyrannized.

It could be argued that this, however regrettable, was an inevitable stage in human evolution. People had reached the stage where through intellect and experiment they were ready to complete the conquest of the laws of the material world. They were ready for full realization, at an increasingly rapid pace, of science and technology. This emphasized the left-brain functions, so patriarchy took over to meet the challenge in the spiritually crudest fashion.

But now the wheel has come full circle. Humankind has essentially discovered the laws of science and technology, and any further development along those lines is simply a matter of building upon foundations already laid. But the mechanical materialism which dominated the race for such knowledge, most markedly in the nineteenth century, is no longer adequate to further progress even in science. The frontiersmen of research, particularly the subnuclear physicists, are increasingly coming up against the facts of multi-level reality, and the best of them are acknowledging this and reacting accordingly.

Patriarchy, having achieved whatever purpose which may have been used (however manipulatively) to justify it, is dying on its feet. It no longer has even a distorted excuse to perpetuate itself—and it had reached the stage where it was emasculating men as well as subjugating women. So rebellion against it is rising, and Paganism, including its Wiccan path, is playing a prominent role in that rebellion.

All that may seem a diversion from the subject of this chapter. Yet it has a direct relevance to it.

Why, for example, is Wicca matriarchal? Why are mainstream covens led by the high priestess, with her high priest working partner rather in the position of a prince consort, equal but secondary? One would think, on the poles-of-a-battery metaphor introduced earlier, that neither one should be "over" the other.

There are two good reasons for this practice. The first is general and essentially timeless. In the philosophy of multi-level reality, the particular strengths of the male and female aspects are found to be emphasized as follows:

Divine Spark – both equal
Spiritual level – female emphasis
Mental level – male emphasis
Astral/psychic level – female emphasis
Physical level – male emphasis

Now it must be admitted that Wiccan working is particularly centered on the spiritual and the astral/psychic levels. This is true of both the religious and the practical (healing, spells, divination, etc.) aspects of that working, what Margaret Murray defined as "ritual witchcraft" and "operative witchcraft." And those two levels are particularly in tune with the feminine aspect of the overall polarity, so it is natural—and more powerful—if both the ritual and the practical work are woman-led.

The mental and physical levels are obviously involved, but as support and in deliberate harmonization with the spiritual and astral/psychic focus. And this is why the male Witches' role is to amplify rather than to lead.

We have found that this principle works in practice as well as in theory. We know personally of at least three covens which were led by a dominantly active high priest, partnered by a high priestess who willingly accepted a secondary role. We liked and respected the people concerned, and their dedication to the Craft was unquestionable. But in all three cases the leading partnerships and the covens themselves in due course fell to pieces and disbanded.

We feel that this reason for the leadership of high priestesses is permanent, but at this point in history it is underlined by a second reason. As patriarchy, and the male-monotheist religious attitudes which reflect it, are messily and reluctantly disintegrating, a practice which emphasizes woman's capabilities, and also reunites the Goddess with her grass-widowed consort, is a positive contribution to progress.

Apart from this matter of high priestess leadership, how is male/female polarity given full scope in mainstream Wiccan practice?

At the time of writing, a spate of "How many so-and-so's does it take to change a light bulb?" jokes are running around Pagandom. One of them asks how many Gardnerian Witches it takes, and the answer is, "Thirteen, composed entirely of equal man-woman partnerships."

Thirteen is an accepted maximum size for a coven (otherwise it becomes depersonalized), not an ideal to be striven for, but the joke does point to the truth that a group-mind of harmonious man-woman working partnerships is indeed worth striving for. If each partnership can achieve the sort of fruitful, and necessarily unique, harmony we have been discussing, and the naturally varied group of partnerships can achieve a more complex harmony among themselves, like the spectrum of a rainbow, the power and effectiveness raised in coven working can be remarkable.

The details of ritual practice emphasize the fundamental polarity. A woman initiates a man, and a man a woman. In a ring dance, or sitting in the ritual circle after the work is over, men and women place themselves alternately, as much as possible. The wine and cakes are consecrated by a man and a woman, and passed woman-to-man, man-to-woman for partaking. Cord magic is performed with a working partnership at opposite ends of each cord, again as far as possible, and so on.

Perhaps the most complex and subtle example of the principle is in the consecration of the wine. This is done by a man holding the chalice and the woman an athame which she dips in the wine while the man voices the ritual blessing.

Now the chalice is a female symbol, and the athame a male one, and their uniting is a "lance and grail" mating. So why are they held that way around?

The answer lies in the levels of reality discussed earlier. The actual blessing of the wine is meant to take effect on the astral/psychic and spiritual levels, so the woman, being more naturally powerful on those levels, activates the "fertilization" by inserting the athame. But the ritual itself is enacted on the physical and mental levels, so as these are his province of emphasis, the man holds the wine and speaks the necessary words.

We must stress once again that all this is a matter of emphasis, not of exclusiveness. The male aspect may be good at organizing spiritual concepts, and the female aspect rightly has an "earthy" reputation, so in these and other ways the level-functions overlap. But in any given situation, such as the consecration of the wine, it is a matter of "aspects of aspects," and each should concentrate on his or her appropriate gifts in the levels involved.

A chapter in this book deals with sex magic in

greater detail, but in the context of what we have discussed here, perhaps we should mention our own attitude to it, which we find is shared by many covens.

Ritual intercourse for magical purposes can certainly raise a great deal of psychic power. Our own rule about it is that it must be practiced only by a married couple or by established lovers of a marriage-like unity, and in private. Witches are not voyeurs.

This rule, quite apart from moral considerations, is based on the fact that sexual intercourse in the intensified atmosphere of a ritual situation involves all the levels from physical to spiritual, and is intended to do so. But sex magic worked (however sincere their motives) by a couple to whom sex is not part of their everyday relationship can have unequal repercussions for each of them and unexpectedly affect more levels in one partner than it does in the other. The purely human dangers of this are obvious, and no couple with respect and compassion for each other would risk them.

Here is an example of successful sex magic from our own history. We moved to Ireland in 1976, having run an active coven in England for more than five years before handing it over to another couple when we left. For our first months in Ireland, we had no coven members except for one already-initiated man who worked many miles away and could rarely visit us. We felt the lack of a group and decided magic was called for.

We cast a ritual circle around our bed with maximum concentration and then made love, envisaging our magical purpose as we did so. At the moment of orgasm we pictured an "astral lighthouse" over our home to attract people of like minds. The very next day, and by a quite unplanned occurrence, we met and were immediate friends with the couple who became our first initiates in Ireland. They were a tower of strength to us while from then on our coven grew steadily.

In terms of psychic resonance, perhaps it was no coincidence that the first people our "lighthouse" attracted were a happily married pair like ourselves. In the normal course of Wiccan growth, they eventually "hived off" and today run their own group in another county.

A final thought: psychic and magical health depends on fruitful communication between the Unconscious and the Conscious. The Unconscious can only speak in symbols while the Conscious expresses itself in deliberately organized thought and speech. So it is not surprising that the Unconscious talks to us most vividly in dreams whose symbols the Conscious can, by intelligent effort, grasp and interpret.

In the other direction, the Conscious can speak to the Unconscious most directly through ritual and drama, which are the enactment of symbolism for a considered purpose. Ritual, consequently, should express the harmony we are trying to achieve within the total psyche, and that, we should never forget, includes the woman's animus and the man's anima.

ABOUT THE AUTHORS

Janet and Stewart Farrar are the authors of seven books on Wicca—*What Witches Do*, *Eight Sabbats for Witches*, *The Witches' Way*, *The Witches' Goddess*, *The Witches' God*, *Life & Times of a Modern Witch*, and *Spells & How They Work*, all of which have been published in British and American editions. Stewart is also the author of seven occult novels, three detective novels and one romance.

Stewart was born June 28, 1916 to an English father

and a Scottish mother. His Sun is in Cancer with Libra rising. He was brought up as a Christian Scientist. He attended the City of London School and University College London, studying journalism at the latter. During World War II, he served in the British Army in the anti-aircraft artillery, ending up with the rank of major. He has been a writer all his life, producing articles, short stories, books, screenplays and radio and television documentary scripts. In 1969 he was sent by the newspaper *Reveille* to interview two prominent English Witches, Alex and Maxine Sanders; becoming interested himself, he was initiated into their London coven in February 1970.

Janet was born June 24, 1950 to a half-English, half-Welsh father and an Irish mother. She is Cancer with Scorpio rising. She was brought up in the Church of England, attended Leyton Manor School, art school, and the Royal Wanstead Boarding School. She worked as a model and receptionist. She was initiated into the Sanders' coven in March 1970; it was there that she and Stewart met.

Stewart and Janet founded their first coven in London on December 22, 1970. They were handfasted on January 31, 1974 and officially married on July 19, 1975, handfasting having no legal status in Britain. They moved to Ireland in 1976 and soon built up a new coven there. Other covens have hived off from that one as well as from their original London group. The Farrars have appeared on Irish and British television and radio, Dutch radio and Spanish television. Their work in Ireland mainly has been devoted to book writing.

Both Janet and Stewart are amateur artists, and Stewart is a semi-professional photographer. They own a dog and four cats.

Janet & Stewart Farrar

Witches and the Earth

by Chas S. Clifton

SUMMER. Wielding their shovels, pulaskis[1] and saws, a Sierra Club trail crew rebuilds a national forest hiking trail on the lower slopes of Pikes Peak. Most of them are people who love the outdoors, contributing a Saturday to a worthwhile project. For one, however, the day will not end when the dusty volunteers carry their litter bags and tools back down to the truck and open the beer cooler. Later that evening, bathed and clothed in special garments, he will be walking up another foothills trail in the twilight. A drummer will precede him; ahead in various clearings will be members of a local coven ready to challenge him with ritual questions. At the ridge top the high priestess will stand, ready to complete his initiation.

AUTUMN. The cool night air makes itself known as the man and woman strip off their clothing by the back-yard hot tub. Handfuls of purifying herbs are scattered on the water's surface. After the ritual bath has transformed them into predators, they dress again: boots, jeans, jackets, hats. Nearby, they encounter a covener wrapped in a blanket, wearing deer antlers. The woman speaks to the "deer," explains their needs, then pretends to fire her rifle at it. That night she sleeps and dreams of two mule deer bucks amid scattered pines. At sunrise three days later two bucks hear movement and quit their browsing. One trots through a shadowy grove of dead ponderosa pine trunks, legacy of a forest fire. The deer pauses; the man braces against a boulder, fires. They carry the deer off the mountain. Later, the skin is given to the one who played a deer in ritual.

WINTER. The temperature falls toward zero. With candles and ritual drama the Sun god dies and is reborn. At one point the coveners leave the ritual room and, alone, each one walks a predetermined course to where the high priest waits by a flowing mineral spring. As each seeker arrives, he offers a short phrase and a sip of the cold, effervescent water, the keynote and the first refreshment of a new solar cycle.

SPRING. Defining his territory, the male broadtailed hummingbird crisscrosses the airspace above the house and garden with whirring wings. The woman walks on the hill behind her house, where a flush of wild onions have popped up in the spring rains. The perennial herbs are growing in her garden; the annual herbs, chile peppers and tomatoes wait to be transplanted. Now, with the sun rising in the sky, she feels her season coming, the time when she feels closest to the earth.

For at least a quarter century we have been told that Wicca—modern Pagan Witchcraft—is an "Earth religion." Modern Pagans like to say that they "celebrate the Earth," and one of the first American Pagan publications was a magazine called *Earth Religion News*, published in the early 1970s. But what is an Earth religion?

First of all, an Earth religion is not focused on preparing the Afterlife. While many Witches refer to something called the Law of Threefold Return, meaning that in
life you get back what you put out, Witchcraft is not devoted to building up good karma, "merit," or building
blocks in a heavenly mansion. We teach that the spirits of
the dead go to a place of rest—the Summerland, the Isles
of the Blessed, call it what you will—but we do not live
our lives as though someone is going to announce a final
score at the end. We say Death is as important and necessary as Life, but we do not say that life is only a long
preparation for death and a "final judgment."

In Witchcraft, this world and this life is not something a person has to be "saved from." We owe it to other
people, other creatures and the planet to be fair, balanced,
honest and not greedy, but we were not born "in sin." We
make mistakes, but no one else paid a debt or made a
sacrifice that will somehow affect our futures or our ad-
ventures in the Afterlife. Nor do we need to be rescued
from our world by benevolent beings from Outer Space.

From the viewpoint of an Earth religion, our bodies
with their appetites, sexuality, and other physical pleas-
ures are not bad or sinful either. We have them for some
purpose, presumably, since our outlook is based on the
belief that the Cosmos is not random, but has pattern and
purpose to it. Consequently, we do need to "free ourselves" from them prematurely. We do not need to "drop
the body" through meditation, "raise its vibrations" by
eating only certain foods, or consider it as all but owned
by Satan, the way some Christians do. The body is not
something that must be ignored or disciplined so that we
can be holy. Our bodies live, then die. They deserve good
care while we have them and careful disposal when no
longer needed. Once dead, they are not going to rise
again in their old forms although their atoms may persist

in new creations.

But as followers—and at times, creators—of an Earth religion, we must decide how we will live in relation to the Earth.

There are many forces today, both obvious and not so obvious, that would force us to ignore the Earth that gave us birth, either by mistreating her directly or by focusing our attention on "spiritual" matters so that we forget her. I have listed a few things that an Earth religion is not; what are some of the things that it is, and how does a Pagan Witch express them?

One of my Craft teachers expressed it this way: Live so that someone ignorant about Paganism would know from watching your life or visiting your home that you followed an "earth religion."

Now it is true that the Latin word *paganus* once meant "country dweller." Via the Roman legions, where it meant something like "dumb hick civilian," it entered early Christian jargon with the meaning of non-believer, someone who had not enlisted in Christ's army. But does its root meaning tell us that all good Pagans should be back-to-the-landers? Not necessarily—although I am all for anyone who can do that successfully without large infusions of outside cash. I myself am happiest in a small town with a big backyard garden and a trout stream ten minutes away, but I have had good experiences in intensely urban environments too. Find your own level— and realize that your needs may be different at different times in your life. But one thing is important wherever you live: *Know where you are.* You cannot love the Earth before you understand something about it. Likewise, you cannot "save the planet" without starting where you are. It is a little hypocritical to be concerned about the fates of species on the other side of the globe before you know what happens to your own take-out pizza cartons after you have disposed of them.

Knowing "where you are" connects with the concept of "bioregions," an attempt to define the way Earth herself is organized—by watersheds and mountain ranges and ecosystems rather than by lines on maps. Back in 1981 the magazine *CoEvolution*, now called *Whole Earth Review*, published a quiz with questions like these[2]:

- Trace the water you drink from precipitation to tap.

- What was the total rainfall in your area last year, July to June?

- What were the primary subsistence techniques of the culture that lived in your area before you?

- Name five edible plants in your region and their seasons of availability.

- How long is the growing season where you live?

- What species have become extinct in your area?

- What is the land history of where you live?

And of course the one I hinted at earlier: Where does your garbage go?

This may not sound like Wicca 101, but perhaps it should be one of the prerequisites. Certainly this kind of basic knowledge would be an antidote to some of the fuzzy, unfocused "heal the Earth" rituals I have found myself in. Magic must be focused to be effective, and the more the magic-worker empathizes with, rationally knows about, and feels the "target," the more likely it will succeed. When someone wants to "heal the Earth" but does not know that the trees surrounding him are lodgepole pine, for instance, I do not think effective magic is being worked. I call that just being a magical tourist.

A key Witchcraft idea is *participation*. We are not what we believe; we are what we do. Likewise, we should participate in the natural processes around us even as we celebrate them abstractly. Participation empowers us: we take control over as many aspects of our lives as possible. This desire to participate in and acknowledge natural cycles is why our festivals connect with the seasonal wheel (see "Seasonal Rites / Magical Rites") rather than re-enacting what some person or group did some centuries ago. This is why Witches traditionally have allied themselves with or themselves been herbalists, midwives, diviners, counselors, and others who helped people heal themselves, control their destinies, and get a handle on their affairs rather than submit to "experts" on high who decreed what medical treatment was legitimate, how many babies a woman was to bear, or how people should "accept what God has given them." The gods, after all, help those who help themselves; that, incidentally, is the justification for "low magic" or "spells."

But as simple as the idea of participating in natural cycles and events may seem, there are powerful cultural forces today working against it. These opposing forces are based in dualism—not just the old Gnostic whispers never purged from Christianity that the "world" is bad and only the "spirit" is good, but modern, secular manifestations of the same concept.

Consider how people react to the idea of the environmental crisis. It is easy to look at some of the horrible things humanity has done to the Earth, with evil effects on its other inhabitants and on us too, and come to the mistaken conclusion that "humans are un-Natural," that we are some sort of cosmic mistake, and that the best thing we could do now is to shrink back from any further contact with the natural world, making our motto, "Look, don't touch." Don't practice agriculture, don't build a fire in the woods, don't pick those herbs, don't graze cattle, don't hunt, don't fish, don't dig up any minerals. This reaction is understandable sometimes, but it is a panic reaction nevertheless, pushed from within by the false dualistic idea (part of our "Western heritage" but now common throughout the industrialized world) that humanity is not part of Nature, but rather some superior "spiritual" race in conflict with physical reality.

The truth is we are a part of Nature and subject to her rules. We might say we get the Nature we deserve, and as the saying goes, Nature bats last. Despite our free will, our ability to store knowledge and create histories, if the Crone Goddess decides we have grown past our limits, then, as the wildlife biologists say, our population will "crash." If some horrible plague sweeps the land, it may not matter who was a Witch, who was a vegetarian, or who gave money to the correct political cause.

To forestall that possibility, the world needs Paganism's pragmatic philosophy. And Pagans themselves need some of the earthy, practical outlook typical of the old-time *paganus*, whether we live in cabins in the woods or high-rise apartments. This comes through participation in nature, as mentioned, and a balanced outlook. It is developed through daily life rather than the occasional grand ritual. Even if we buy most of our bread in a store, we reconnect with the true meaning of the festival of Lammas, for example, by growing some grain (for my household it is blue Indian corn), harvesting and grinding it, and baking with the flour. Hanging on the workshop wall all winter, the best blue ear reminds us of the cycle; its kernels will be planted the next spring. If one's own or a community garden is unavailable, grow herbs or vegetables in pots; it is the using of them that makes the practice worthwhile.

Similarly, killing and dressing our own meat—at least occasionally—can open the way to the understanding of the universal cycle of death expressed by the festival of Samhain.

Even in its attenuated, commercialized form of Halloween, this old Pagan holiday has power because we live in a culture that likes to pretend death never comes. When we participate in death with reverence and understanding, we realize that while the energy that powers life is transferred, no one organism owns it. We take; we give back. Indeed, if there are problems concerned with hunting or animal husbandry, they are not the faults of our natures but of our numbers, signs that (in some regions at least) we are too crowded like caged lions in a zoo, unable to lead authentic human lives our ancestors would recognize.

Rather than offer specific magical rituals, I would like to suggest these things: Before we can care for where we are, we have to know where we are. We have to inhabit a particular place—possibly not for our entire lives, but with all possible understanding while we are in that particular place. In understanding the natural order of that particular place, we can begin to create our own spiritual order. "Understanding" is not only a mystical process, but a rational one, using all our human abilities to organize information—call them history, science, culture, art, whatever. From this "earthy" or ecological grounding can develop a truer Pagan culture and community, stronger magic, and a clear-eyed journey on the Witch's path.

ABOUT THE AUTHOR

Born in 1951, Chas S. Clifton grew up in western South Dakota and Colorado. From childhood on he always felt there was some mystery in nature beyond what he learned in school and church; consequently, he was drawn to the Craft while a college student and afterwards. In 1988 he completed a master's degree in religious studies with an emphasis on the development of new religious movements as part of preparation for more writing on Western esoteric traditions. He lives in the Upper Arkansas Valley of Colorado.

NOTES

[1] Combining the functions of an ax and a mattock or grubbing tool, the pulaski is used mainly by forest fire-fighters and trail builders.

[2] The complete quiz appears in Stephanie Mills, *What Ever Happened to Ecology?* San Francisco: Sierra Club Books, 1989, p. 150.

The Solo Witch

by Heather O'Dell

Under a full Moon the woman crosses the meadow, listening to the swish of silvered grasses as they brush against her legs. She stops in a circle of oak trees, her whole being focused on muted sounds, on the smell and feeling of night air against her face. The Moon spills its milky light on her shoulders; she begins to move in a circle. Slowly, heavily, as if rooted within the Earth she moves, singing softly, creating a magical space around her ...

In a city miles away a man walks into a sanctuary he has created, closing the door behind him. Incense obliterates city smells; street sounds diminish. Finally there is only the sound of his breathing. Candles illuminate his ritual tools: athame (ritual knife), chalice, and other objects arranged before him on an altar. In the flickering light he moves through the phrases of his ritual: "This is a time that is not a time, in a place that is not a place ... "

In cities and rural areas everywhere women and men go alone to celebrate the Pagan festivals. Solitary Witches by chance or by choice, we practice our religion just as coven members do. In some ways we must work a little harder, explore some blind alleys, fight some personal demons along the way, but the result can be worth the extra trouble.

You do not have to belong to a coven to acquire the knowledge you need to be a Witch, to work magic, create powerful rituals and experience the wonder of a life lived in celebration. You can explore the mysteries of the cosmos and of your psyche, returning with treasures of self-reliance and self-knowledge. And far from being lonely, you can use your strengths to form connections of friendship and service, building a community around you.

Certainly there are disadvantages. If you are already a practicing solitary Witch, you are well aware of them. For example:

You do not have a ready-made group with which to celebrate rituals. With a group, a feast can be more festive. There are more voices to sing, more bodies to dance, more colors, laughter, hands to touch and usually more wonderful plates of food from which to eat afterwards. If everything is working right, a tremendous amount of power is generated; you know that magic is in the air.

You lack the special companionship that covens can offer. Of course you want to share your thoughts and experiences with others who "speak the same language," who know just what you mean when you describe your plans for Candlemas or how you found your athame or exactly how you felt the circle build around you that last time. You may want to seek or give advice that is not couched in the terms of someone else's religion or the newest psycho-babble. You may simply long for the heightened bond that can exist between individuals who share Wiccan spirituality as well as other facets of life.

You cannot rely on someone else for motivation. Left on its own, your enthusiasm can be all but extinguished under the weight of everyday stress and cares, illness or just plain boredom—just when you need it most. The intellect is willing, but the spirit has taken a vacation; it is easier to turn on the television or curl up with a novel than to create a ritual. A group's psychic energy can jump-start your flagging enthusiasm, get you started when you thought you would never start and keep you going when it seems like an uphill struggle.

You may find it difficult to be objective. As Witches we are constantly exploring uncharted areas: the realms of magic and the mind. What we find sometimes confuses us or even scares us. It helps to have others to furnish us with an objective viewpoint or an experience against which to compare ours. On our own we face a risk of getting lost in tangles of subjectivity.

There is no Craft teacher right there with you. If you are alone and new to the Craft, you may be overwhelmed by all that you think you must learn. The many books seem to present a bewildering array of information to the newcomer and—especially when it comes to the specifics of ritual—may seem to contradict one another. No one can blame you for wanting to join an experienced coven, to have a safe haven where you can practice and learn under the direction of others who have integrated and used all this information in a way that works.

For all the problems of going it alone, however, being a solitary Witch has some advantages. Consider the compensations afforded solo practitioners:

You are better off on your own than in the wrong coven. Suppose you are drawn to the feminist traditions and find the only coven available in your area to be one led by a dogmatic high priest whose practice—in your eyes—is patterned too closely on one of the patriarchal religions. (Covens like these do exist!) What if you prefer to improvise your rituals while other coveners never deviate from the procedure set down in someone's *Book of Shadows*, or conversely what if your preference for form and continuity is constantly sabotaged by those around you who seem to thrive on anarchy? Or what if you simply have nothing in common other than your religion with other Pagans in your community? In the intimate, family-like coven setting, this can be a real drawback for the "different" member. Alone, you can work and celebrate as you please, when you please and (assuming you like yourself) in congenial company.

You are not bothered by distractions. Most people find it easiest to concentrate when alone, and concentration is vital to good magic. But even in the most harmonious company you may find yourself swayed from your intention by the sheer force of group energy or interrupted in your mental imagery by a comment or inadvertent noise from someone else.

You can always act when the time is right. In magic as in sex, timing is all-important. The time of day, your own special rhythm, Moon phase or weather may be crucial to accomplishing your magical intention, and rarely will a group's timing perfectly match your own. Inspiration, the kind that suddenly dissolves all boundaries, is fragile and elusive as a minute. If you ignore it until your group finishes discussing last month's ritual or the appropriate way to "call the quarters," you may lose it.

You learn to rely on yourself. Working alone in the Craft—searching for answers within yourself and from outside, striving to integrate your spirituality into your daily life and relationships, learning to trust your perceptions, intuitions and reactions—you can develop a degree of self-reliance that is hard to attain within the shelter (and confines!) of a group. The admonition, "Know thyself," is timeless and universal. As Ralph Waldo Emerson said in his essay "Self-Reliance," "Nothing is at last sacred but the integrity of your own mind." Knowing ourselves, relying on ourselves, we develop inner reserves from which to draw when we or others need to. Witches are reminded how important self-reliance is when we repeat the Charge of the Goddess:

> *And you who think to seek for me,*
> *know that your seeking and yearning*
> *shall avail you not*
> *unless you know the mystery:*
> *That if that which you seek*
> *you find not within you,*
> *you will never find it without you.*
> *For behold, I have been with you*
> *from the beginning*
> *and I am that which is attained*
> *at the end of desire.*

Living the Craft as a Solitary

When you blend your spirituality with the cadence of your life and live the Craft from day to day, you come to appreciate solo practice's benefits and minimize its shortcomings. The quality of our Craft derives more from what we put into it—commitment, work, a sense of wonder, a willingness to share what we have learned—than from any coven affiliation.

If you are new to the Craft and alone, or if you are already practicing but find something missing, here are some suggestions for solitary practice. First, read. Read books on understanding dreams, astrology, meditation techniques, parapsychology. Read about the history of Witchcraft and its practice today, about myths from different cultures, and herbal medicine. Read fact and read fiction: let one source lead you to another in a treasure hunt for knowledge. I will admit to a personal prejudice here: I cannot imagine my world without books. But beyond that, I have found that most people drawn to the Craft are addicted to reading. It is rare to find a modern Witch without also finding a houseful of books.

Keep a dream journal and record everything you remember about your dreams: color and feeling and waking associations as well as the dream sequence itself. Look to your dreams for messages and inspiration. Play with your dreams. Act out the parts of various dream images, both animate and inanimate. Draw a picture of your dream; transform it into your personal myth; build a ritual around it. Not only will you learn from your dreams, but you will find that close attention to that other world you enter in sleep will imbue your waking hours with an aura of enchantment.

If you want to work magic you must learn mental discipline. Choose the meditation technique that suits you best and practice it daily. Learn to find that quiet place inside yourself where wisdom speaks—and listen. Cultivate the art of visualization. Without the ability to visualize, your rituals will be merely theater, not complete magical workings.

A Witch must learn to hear his or her inner voice through dreamwork and mental exercise, but the physical senses need exercising too. The Craft, after all, is an earth religion. We work with powers of Air, Fire, Water and Earth: observe these forces as they occur in the world around you so that you will know them in your heart. Notice how sounds travel on the wind, and how the air changes day to day, place to place. Take a long, slow breath.

Open your palms to the Sun's heat. Watch its light fill hidden corners of the landscape and change the color of the sky. Wade in a stream or the ocean and feel the water's force. Watch it move.

Gather a handful of soil and feel its temperature and texture against your skin. Smell it when it is wet; compare that to its smell when dry. Gardening is great way to observe all the elements. Plant some herbs and watch them sprout and grow, responding to light and water. (If you have no garden, plant them in pots.) Feel their leaves; smell them. Taste them. Learn their uses in magic and in healing.

Remember that your body is sacred too and attend to its well-being. Swim, run or walk. Practice T'ai Chi or Hatha Yoga. Move as much as you are able. Choose nourishing food and prepare it with love, then savor it.

Practicing Solitary Witchcraft

Solitary ritual work does not have to be dreary. Alone you can carry out ritual that is powerful, effective and just right for you. You may chose from a script in a book, re-enact one you learned or create your own. The beauty of solo ritual lies in your freedom to fashion it just as you want.

In adapting a group ritual to solo, you will probably want to simplify it and make it less wordy. In a group, the theatrical presentation is usually more effective, so when working alone, you may find it better to substitute intense visualization for much of the speaking and action of

Photo © 1991 Malcolm Brenner / Eyes Open

group ceremonial. But if you wish to add a poem, chant or dance, you can. Search within yourself to find what your-deepest Self responds to. Lift aside the curtain of your dreams. Listen to your body and your heart; translate what you hear into motion. You may this way touch the sacred more surely than you could in all but the most developed group simply because you have put more of yourself into your magic.

However you decide to carry out your ritual and spellcasting, you will probably want to follow the basic structure of modern Craft ceremonies. What follows is a short description of ceremonial structure, followed by a solo self-initiation ritual. If you are standing at the thresh-old of declaring yourself a Witch, you may wish to study this part carefully, then perform it at the first good oppor-tunity.

Purification. Before you start any ritual, set aside time to shed emotional baggage that will distract you from total involvement. No magic works when you enter your circle burdened with leftover anger or worry; this is one of the most important principles. To symbolize your purification, try bathing by candlelight, adding cleansing herbs such as sage, cedar, rosemary or lavender to the water. Or lie in a rushing stream, or build a sweat bath and burn sage. However you purify yourself, you must feel all preoccupations "washed away." Follow that with a short meditation until you feel the quiet place inside you where there is only serenity.

Casting the circle. The circle marks the area for ritual working. It sets off the mundane world from the timeless, spaceless point that becomes magic's setting. The power you build in ritual, gaining intensity as it spirals around you, is contained by the circle. Traditionally a Witch moves clockwise when casting a circle, the direction in which the (Northern Hemisphere) Sun appears to move above us, denoting a gathering-in of power. The circle is oriented to the four cardinal directions which in turn symbolize the magical elements of Air, Fire, Water and Earth.

Invoking the Goddess and the God. In invoking the Goddess and the God we become them for a time. We experience that part of ourselves that is divine. We call for the feminine and masculine powers—dark and light, generating and dying, searching and sheltering—that each of us contains, repeating in our ritual the act of creation made by the joining and separating of these divine forces. When that power is felt, whether you have invoked it by words, thoughts, songs, dance or mental imagery, then magic can be worked.

Self-Initiation

Through initiation we express our commitment to the Craft (and in groups, a formal acceptance by the coven). Initiation is an essential step the solo practitioner should not skip. It becomes a powerful expression of your transition into Witchcraft.

Initiation takes you from death to your old life to rebirth in a new one. You die to some old attitudes and ways of being in the world and are born to living the Craft. You enter the darkness of your unconscious, listening for the voice of inner direction, relinquishing dependence on old authorities as you move toward the light of your own true nature. Carefully planned and carried out, your personal initiation ceremony can effect a powerful transformation in your life.

A close friend of mine, who carried out a ritual similar to the one below when he decided as a young man to follow the Craft, described it as more powerful than he had expected merely reading the printed words beforehand. As he moved through the ritual, he said, he was unexpectedly hit by an uneasy feeling that white-bearded Jehovah would indeed be angered by his defection and strike him dead, even though he had not consciously considered himself a Christian for a decade. But by the time he had finished the short ritual, he knew he was a Witch, with all vestiges of his childhood religion's "authority" put away from him. He has never turned back.

That which follows is a simple self-initiation ritual. Use it as a starting place from which to build your own.

To define your ritual area, place candles at what will be the north, east, south and west points of your circle. Place an altar candle on a flat surface such as a rock or table. Near the altar candle arrange a small container of anointing oil (either prepared ritual oil or simply pure olive oil), another of incense or fragrant herbs to burn, and some wine in a cup or chalice. If you have other personal items that are important to you, such as your athame (ritual knife), magical jewelry, or a "medicine bag," put them on the altar too.

If possible, schedule this ritual at the full Moon on a day when you can be alone. Spend that day quietly, perhaps walking outdoors or listening to music—some activity that will encourage a meditative state. Then prepare for ritual by slowly bathing in water to which you have added the appropriate herbs and/or oils. When you leave the bath, leave all preoccupations—along with your clothing—behind. Nude ("skyclad," as Witches say), enter the ritual space as though you were entering a world you have never known before.

Light a candle and take a few minutes to feel its warmth on your body and to watch its moving light. Ig-

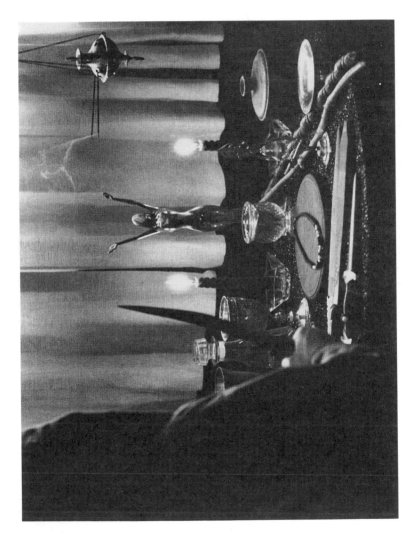

nite your incense.

Carrying the anointing oil, move to the east quarter and light the candle there. Touch the oil to your forehead, your eyelids, lips, hands, breast, genitals and feet, saying in turn, "My mind, my eyes, my lips, my hands, my breast, my sex, my feet." Visualize a wind from the east breathing life into each of the body points you have anointed.

Move to the south quarter, lighting that candle. Repeat the anointing and self-blessing, visualizing the Sun's heat from the south building vitality and passion at each point you touch.

Move to the west quarter and light that candle. This time, feel the fluids in your body as they flow through each of the spots you anoint.

Move to the north quarter and light that candle. As you repeat the anointing and self-blessing, visualize the earthy, enduring substance of your body at each of the spots you touch.

Returning to your altar, anoint your body as before one more time, very slowly and consciously. As you do so, say:

> *Be with me, Goddess and God.*
> *With my mind and imagination*
>   *I will seek to understand Your mysteries.*
> *With my eyes I will see the beauty of the Earth.*
> *My lips will speak of You*
>   *in music and language,*
>   *and my hands will do Your work.*
> *With my breast I will give comfort;*
>   *my sex will express joy in new life.*
> *And always in Your ways my feet will travel.*

(You may substitute any divine names you wish.)

Slowly drink the wine from your chalice, savoring it. Then hold the chalice up in front of you and say, "I, (give your Craft name if you have chosen one), am a Witch."

Community. Just because you are a solitary Witch does not mean you must be a lonely one. You are neglecting an important part of the Craft if you hug it to yourself, turning your energy always inward instead of allowing it to radiate into the world around you. Remember, the Craft is an earth religion: everyone and everything is sacred. Contribute to and partake of this sacredness by sharing your gifts and knowledge. The people around you can benefit from your abilities as an astrologer or an herbalist or a storyteller or a carrier of groceries. Every person you meet can use your compassion at one time or another, as can plants, animals and the Earth that supports you. Strengthen your connection with the Goddess and God by strengthening the bond between you and the world.

You have a community, and it is all around you. You almost certainly will encounter people, both Craft and otherwise, who share your interest and possess similar talents. Others will be able to fill in where your knowledge is weak. In associating with these people and with those who need your help you will learn and grow, just as you would in any coven. In fact, as a solitary Witch you will be unlikely to fall into the habit of confining your "community" to fellow coveners. By opening your circle of friendship you will discover that there is indeed richness in diversity.

When you want to make contact with others in the Craft, you will find it is increasingly easy to do so. Pagan festivals are proliferating all around the United States and some foreign countries. The best way to find them is through Pagan publications. (Some reliable ones are listed in the last chapter.) Bring your tent and some food and be prepared to meet like-spirited people who just might become lifelong friends.

One day when I was a child, I sat on a grassy bank in the woods, listening to a symphony played by robins and wood thrushes, rustling maple leaves above me and the rush of Willow Creek below me. It was late spring and the smell of new vegetation was sweet on the air. No one else was there to distract me with words; this one time everything I saw, felt, smelt and heard was there for me only. It was one of the happiest moments of my life. Later I painted the scene as I remembered it: a solitary girl in the woods. I titled it "Alone." The painting won first prize in a school contest, which pleased me, but some viewers' reactions did not. "How sad," they said. "She looks so lonely." It seemed futile to protest this misconception, and so I did not, just as now I ignore those coven Witches who think my life is somehow less complete than theirs. Instead, I find joy as a solitary practitioner, knowing that while it may not be the best for everyone, it is the only way for me. I can be a Witch alone. And so can you.

ABOUT THE AUTHOR

Heather O'Dell lives in Colorado where she tends a large garden and a cluster of cats. This is her first contribution to a book-length work.

Witchcraft and the Law

by Pete Pathfinder

Witchcraft! Pagan worship rites! Right here in River City! Such ideas titillate, annoy or even outrage some— but by no means all—mainstream religious Americans. The thought of open, public Wiccan and Pagan religious ceremonies is also seen with indignation and outrage by some conservative or traditionalist modern Pagans.

Non-Pagans can for the most part be forgiven for their attitudes since they arise from misinformation and ignorance. But I have trouble forgiving the Wiccan and Pagan ultra-conservatives, those bent on keeping the Old Religion and its teachings secret except to a chosen few. They may be part of the problem rather than the solution to the Old Religion's public-relations woes.

In times past our religion was kept alive by small close-knit groups meeting necessarily secretly, since discovery meant torture and death at the hands of oppressors. Nonetheless, the Old Religion survived 500 years of murderous oppression to be reborn in the 20th century, healthy and growing. While the Christian church was unsuccessful in snuffing out the sometimes weak flame of Pagan belief, it managed to force us into a structure that would stymie our growth for a long time: the small, family-like coven. Over the last 25 years various Pagans have attempted to create larger organized groups, but always on the same model, the coven. Virtually all have failed.

A group's dynamics change drastically when the group gets larger than 25 or so, and again around 75, and again near 200. The published research on group dynamics is worth reading by anyone interested in creating larger Pagan worship groups. The coven model, though it works well in smaller situations, does not work with larger groups, so we need to rethink our structure if we would create larger, open "churches." We might consider studying our competitors and learning from their successes.

While forming formal "churches" is still a relatively new process in Paganism, it has occurred in the United States, Canada and a number of other English-speaking countries. The 1980s saw an upsurge in groups conducting large, semi-public gatherings all across the U.S., pretty much independently of and often unaware of each other. The Covenant of Unitarian Universalist Pagans (CUUPS) is a prime example. In fact, because of its institutional roots, CUUPS is free from two major problems affecting Pagan organizers: how to secure recognition from government agencies and how to find a large enough site to accommodate all those who want to worship together.

Unfortunately, the public image we have created by being secretive works against our acceptance as a religion. By being secretive, we send the nonverbal message that we ourselves are not comfortable with what we are doing. Naturally people assume that this is because we are doing something bad.

Nevertheless, the U.S. Constitution and—for those in other countries—the United Nations Declaration of Human Rights make it clear that government is to be our defender rather than our oppressor. Make no mistake, while it may often be necessary to remind some small-minded bureaucrats who try to deny us our rights of the fact, and even though the government may at times be an unwilling defender, it is our defender nonetheless. Our right to freedom of worship is guaranteed; we need only stand up and demand it. Rights historically have been secured for us by those who were willing to stand and fight for them, and today's situation is no different.

In 1979 a small group of Seattle-area Pagans decided to form a legal church organization, known as the Aquarian Tabernacle Church (ATC). It has existed quietly and without high profile more than a decade at this writing, holding open worship rites on the sabbats and new Moons at our retreat house in the nearby mountains. For those early years the ATC was content to have incorporated as a church, having applied for and received an Internal Revenue Service letter of determination recognizing our non-taxable status. Beyond that, we avoided contact with mainstream religious organizations.

In 1989, however, a Seattle television news program implied that the ATC was connected with Satanic and criminal doings, an event which forced us to become completely open and public in order to make our case known. Because we were being ignored, we found it necessary to ask the mainstream religious groups for help in our confrontation with the television station. Much to our amazement, we got it! While it was not without some hesitation and reservations on the part of a few, we were able to build sturdy bridges to Christian, Jewish, and interfaith organizations and now participate in regional religious federations such as the Interfaith Council and the

Church Council. We opened channels of frank discussion leading to our acceptance as representatives of a valid spiritual tradition. We were even successful in getting Wicca included as an accepted religion in the Washington state prison system with its own section in the chaplain's manual.

Some Christian clergy, no doubt, are convinced in their own minds that we are going to their Hell in a handbasket, but they are courteous enough to keep the thought to themselves and not bother us with it. All in all, we in the ATC are treated with respect and now have the opportunity to educate them about the Old Religion and to do away with the old stories they have heard about malevolent witches, flying broomsticks, and all of that nonsense.

Ironically, the ATC has been criticized more by some of our fellow Pagans for participating in these interfaith groups. Some Pagan leaders must feel threatened in the hold they have over their groups by a possible loss of secrecy! If you are a public Pagan, be prepared for some attacks from your own.

The key to our approach is that it is easier to educate the leaders than the followers. Educating the followers is too large a job, and it's likely they won't believe us anyway. But if we can inform their leaders, the clergy, then perhaps the masses will follow their lead. The only reason people harass us is because they believe they are carrying out the will of their deity. If their clergy tells them that it is wrong to harass us, they will stop doing it sooner than if we try to tell them ourselves. The clergy, frankly, are more likely to respond to the moral obligation to seek the truth.

The same thing is true when dealing with government agencies. Instead of waiting for the police to raid an outdoor worship site after a call from a frightened neighbor who is certain that "dark doings" are afoot, we must take the initiative. Contact the commander of the local police precinct, sheriff's station, or state patrol station *ahead of time*. Go to their office suitably dressed for business and armed with some literature, pamphlets and a list of reliable sourcebooks, such as those by Margot Adler or Rev. Gordon Melton. Provide a brief overview of the religion and of the particular rite you intend to perform.

Rehearse what you will say, leave out nothing important, but do not go into *too much* detail and confuse them. They will probably be somewhat uncomfortable about your visit, and so will you, but be confident, organized, thorough and above all, matter-of-fact and businesslike. Invite them to view the site or perhaps a rehearsal of the rite. Then when the call comes in from the frantic neighbor who sees flickering candles in the woods and hears faint chanting, the police will explain that what is happening is a religious expression instead of raiding your worship with flashing lights and sirens. You have the right to do what you are doing, and the authorities will be happy to know that ahead of time to avoid inappropriate reactions and unnecessary involvement in your exercise of your constitutional rights.

While some people in government may want to force their own beliefs on the world, most are aware of the constitutional rights we all enjoy and would rather not get involved in such issues. But if they do interfere, help is absolutely necessary. Should you sense trouble ahead, make contact with the American Civil Liberties Union, a local Interfaith Council if one exists, or the well-known Jewish religious-rights group, the B'nai B'rith Anti-Defamation League. Explain your activities and ask for their help should a confrontation arise.

Making Your Church Legal

While an unincorporated body can get by with a set of articles of association, incorporating as a non-profit, tax-exempt "church" is best. It is relatively inexpensive ($25 in Washington state, for example), and you can prepare the necessary documents and file them yourself without a lawyer if your budget won't allow one. IRS Publication 557, "Tax-Exempt Status for Your Organization," which is available free, gives sample articles of incorporation and articles of association containing the specific language required in order to receive IRS recognition as tax-exempt. Your library may be able to supply additional books on self-incorporation.

From the beginning of the process, group finances must be handled and recorded properly with no individual profiting from incorporating as a church. Any attempts to form a church as some type of personal tax shelter are ultimately doomed to failure and may expose their operators to large fines or prison terms. In addition, any such scandal hurts the entire Pagan community, something we can do without in this time of relative infancy and vulnerability.

Once you have incorporated as a nonprofit organization, you will need to get an IRS "Letter of Determination" which confirms your additional tax-exempt status. (It is possible to be nonprofit without being tax-exempt.). A fee is charged by the IRS for this filing, so you will need the help of a lawyer and/or certified public accountant at this stage. Having that letter in hand will dispel all questions as to your legitimacy in the eyes of other religious organizations and government agencies. Even with professional help, it may take a year or more to get the Letter of Determination. Don't despair. If it is denied, apply again and keep re-applying. Or if you are not able to afford long, drawn out legal processes, affiliate with a larger group which like the ATC has already secured a group exemption letter. In either case, your church will have to operate within accepted accounting principles. Later, a group exemption can be the springboard from which to seek your own determination letter.

With the letter, you can get nonprofit bulk mailing rates, exemption from sales tax for church supplies in some states, and if your church actually owns real estate, exemption from property tax.

Dealing with the News Media

From a journalistic standpoint, the real story in Paganism is simply that the average person's perception of our religion is so far from the truth as to be ridiculous. Consequently, what we really do is interesting because it is so different from what people think we do. Because of Paganism's growth and its relationship to the feminist movement, editors and news directors are beginning to find us interesting at times of the year other than Halloween. Most editors and reporters are objective and fair, but some let their standards slip when dealing with "fringe movements," so you will need to take some precautions.

First, avoid confrontational broadcasts that seek to create a debate between opposing philosophies. The producers want a lot of shouting to keep things interesting to viewers, but these shows can become quite abusive, particularly off-camera. Why be someone's afternoon entertainment? It is too hard to make your point in a confrontational setting, so these programs are better avoided. If anyone wants to do a news story about us that is sensitive and objective, we should help them all we can, but if they just want to pit us against close-minded antagonists, we can find better things to do with our time.

Overall, when dealing with the news media as a representative Pagan, you will fare best if you set the tone of the interview yourself by asking for agreement to some simple ground rules. If the reporter or photographer does not agree, end it there unless you enjoy being manipulated.

1. Make it clear that you are accepting them as authorized representatives of their employers and will hold them personally responsible for their employers honoring the agreements you make. If they say they are not authorized to make such agreements, call a halt to the interview until they can produce someone with the authority to agree.

2. If you or some of your group do not want to be photographed, stipulate in advance that no photographs of any kind may be published or aired without the permission of anyone identifiable in them. You should be aware that group activities in public places (such as city parks) that are normally visible to passers-by may be photographed by anyone for any legitimate purpose; the general rule is that individual rights to privacy diminish as the depicted group's size increases. On private property, if you are concerned about security from vandals or anything similar, make sure that no photographs of buildings or terrain features that might identify the location are made.

3. Remember that our faith persisted for many years in secrecy and does not depend on publicity to exist. Remember too that *no* publicity is better than *bad* publicity and that you are helping them to earn their salaries with little in return but the satisfaction of telling the truth.

Therefore, before the interview, explain diplomatically that because the reporter is not really familiar with the dividing line between folk myth and the facts of our religion, you would like to read a final draft of the article or see the video to point out anything they may have misinterpreted. Make it clear that your intent is not to exercise creative control, which they would not allow anyway, but is limited to commenting on inadvertent errors or misrepresentations. Point out that your comments are non-binding and they can always do what they want to afterwards. Some journalists may take this as an insult to their integrity (and possibly as an indication that you are hiding something), but insist on it anyway. It is the only way you can be assured of being quoted in the proper contexts and getting fair treatment.

This is a form of insurance. If you have had a chance to object to something, there remains no defense for using it as written should you feel compelled to sue later on, and they know it.

If you cannot get this agreement, go no further unless you trust the reporter enough to let him or her decide on matters he or she may not fully comprehend. Newspeople are under constant pressure to fill pages and air time, and this can make some reporters inadvertently insensitive when gathering quotes or sound and video "bites." Avoid becoming a "media junkie"—sometimes no news is good news.

4. One way to avoid problems associated with item number three is to provide good background materials. This is valuable if your area has been affected by "ritual crime" hysteria or Satanism hype. At these times it is important to make contact with the police, as described above, and the press to let them know who and what you are and what you *are not*. Good materials are available from the Center for Non-Traditional Religion, the Church of All Worlds, Circle, Covenant of the Goddess, Witches'

Anti-Defamation Lobby and elsewhere. (See "Additional Resources.")

I find it useful to send three separate copies of the background materials packet to each media organization I am dealing with: one to the general manager or managing editor, one to the news editor or news director, and here is the important one: one to their general legal counsel. The last one is best sent by certified mail with a return receipt requested. Address each person by his or her name and title, which you can get by a telephone call to the business's receptionist. Keep the return receipt as proof the attorney received the documents, for should any impropriety arise, foreknowledge ignored can constitute malice, the basis for a successful defamation or libel suit. Include with each mailing a polite cover letter with return addresses and telephone numbers. Keep the tone positive, trusting and upbeat. And do not assume that telling your newspaper or television station the truth about the Craft once will do the trick—it won't! I cannot over-emphasize that blanketing the news media at all levels, over and over again, every year until you are completely satisfied with their objectivity and knowledge, is very important.

When you do see a story or broadcast that misrepresents us, respond with a firm, factual explanation of the inaccuracies, including your "press packet." Spare them your outrage: instead, try to arrange a meeting between representatives of your group and them, without any lawyers, to discuss any serious inaccuracies. Never assume malice in anything that can more easily be attributed to stupidity.

Avoid threatening to sue or having a lawyer contact them except as a last resort. Once that happens, the paper or station will become intransigent. Libel suits are expensive and usually decided in favor of the press if only on appeal. In the long run, outrage will do less to improve the behavior of the news media than patiently informing them of the facts. Consider the situation as an opportunity to develop a rapport that will prove useful later on. Finally, whether conducting your own religious organization's business, dealing with law-enforcement officials or dealing with the news media, remember the words of Dr. Albert Schweitzer: "Example is not the main thing in influencing others; it is the *only* thing."

ABOUT THE AUTHOR

Pete Pathfinder was born on the vernal equinox in 1937. With a Roman Catholic father and Pagan mother, he was raised in the Catholic church until his interest in Paganism was awakened in his late teens. Before moving to the Pacific Northwest, he served his hometown in New Jersey as a councilman, police constable and mayor. After moving to Seattle he worked in the electronic-security industry. For many years a self-identified Wiccan, he studied with various teachers before being moved to form the Aquarian Tabernacle Church (ATC) in 1979. Based in the English tradition, the ATC operates an open facility where Pagans of all positive paths can meet together for monthly esbats and the eight major holidays. The ATC is recognized as a tax-exempt church by the state and federal governments and participates in local and international religious networks. Pete was also the Covenant of the Goddess's first elected public-information spokesman, preparing that international Wiccan group's first press packet. He is Wiccan advisor to the Washington State Department of Corrections Religious Program.

Bone Beaters: Witchcraft and Shamanism

by Grey Cat

A shaman[1] lives in two worlds, the ordinary world of objective reality and the invisible world of the gods, spirits, totems and ancestors. The shaman is a "master of death, he actually dies and is actually reborn."[2] He is a traveler to realms not visible to the ordinary person and he attains a relationship with "spirits." Through this relationship he controls these spirits and obtains their help with the concerns of those around him (or her). The anthropologist Michael Harner described a shaman as "a man or woman who enters an altered state of consciousness—at will—to contact and utilize an ordinarily hidden reality in order to acquire knowledge, power and to help other persons."[3] Anthropologists see shamans as operating in a tribal context: a fairly stable group of people who strongly identify as "us" and see those outside the group as "them."

Many Witches today say that "those we call Witches were the tribal shamans of pre-Christian Europe."[4] "Like many other regions, Europe had an indigenous, tribal, shamanic tradition. Today, we claim that tradition for our own."[5] There are of course dissenting voices: "The fact that ... some magical techniques we now call 'shamanic' had become part of the folk magic traditions of many European tribes doesn't 'make' the Witches 'really' shamans either."[6]

Possible parallels between European magical traditions and the shamanism anthropologists described elsewhere in the world puzzled religion historian Mircea Eliade, who wrote:

> If the word "shaman" is taken to mean any magician, sorcerer, medicine man, or ecstatic found throughout the history of religions and religious ethnography, we arrive at a notion at once extremely complex and extremely vague; it seems, furthermore, to serve no purpose, for we already have the terms "magician" or "sorcerer" to express notions as unlike and as ill-defined as "primitive magic" or "primitive mysticism."[7]

So without going into the "real" sources of modern Witchcraft, we must answer two questions: can there be shamans outside of "primitive" culture and can there be shamans outside of tribal culture?

Well, what *is* primitive culture? Until recently anthropologists defined it as the absence of "civilization," in other words, no complex social systems, jobs and bosses, monetary exchange, and the supposedly more sophisticated monotheistic religious view. However, doubts have arisen as to whether this definition was any more than an expression of those researchers' need to define themselves as superior to the cultures under study.

As to the "tribal" question, the answer could be taken as no. Modern Witches in North America or other industrialized countries do not constitute a tribe as usually defined. But to some extent, because of prejudice and consequent "them" and "us" attitudes, added to deliberate attempts to promote a form of tribalism, it might apply.

Shamanism is a technique, not a religion. The shaman is not every priest, medicine man, healer or magician. Rather, the shaman is a magical specialist, as is the ritual leader or the diviner with cards or astrologer. The fact that a shaman may or may not be a priest only makes people who like things to be in neat categories uncomfortable. The shaman is defined by the way he or she works: seeking the ecstasy of the spirit journey, seeking needed answers from those who live in the Other World, but living at once in both worlds.

Classical shamanism as defined by historians of religion and anthropologists always included a "near-death experience." A serious illness or accident in childhood or young adulthood often signaled the future shaman's career. In other cases when a person became a shaman by choice or family succession, the near-death experience was deliberately caused.

Tied to that and subsequent experiences was the shamanic vision. What interested me was that comparable visions have been reported from different peoples in different lands. A Lakota Sioux, a Yakut Eskimo and a South American Jivaro might all experience the vision of a cave opening up in front of the visionary. Entering it, they reported similar experiences. Shamans' visions included changing to an animal's shape, seeing one's own bones, speaking to ancestors and seeing the rainbow bridge between all peoples. That the hidden cave opened up in the ice for one visionary and in a sand dune for another was only a difference in detail.

However shamanism is packaged, one thing is of key importance. A shaman exists in relation to his or her community. A hermit who speaks to no one is not a shaman although he may be a mystic. A person who attends an expensive workshop on shamanism to gain self-understanding is not a shaman until she uses it to help people around her. A true shaman may sacrifice personal survival in order to help the community he or she is called to. "Having the vision" does not make a shaman by itself.

A second key indicator of shamanism is the use of the altered state or trip to the Other World. The shaman controls this process: he goes into it when there is a job to do and can find his way out when the needed information is obtained. Whether going to the Underworld or flying to perch on the World Tree, the shaman knows the destination and what will be found there. Shamans are not trance mediums or "channels" who need someone else to record their words while in trance; they bring back their information consciously.

A controversial element of classical shamanism is many shamans' use of powerful mind-altering drugs. Some people consider use of such drugs *the* indicator of true shamanism, but I feel this is too narrow a definition. The work of Mircea Eliade and other scholars makes it clear that drugs were not ubiquitous in shamanic practice.

Are modern Wiccans the inheritors of prehistoric European shamanism? Having examined the published British Gardnerian materials and interviewed Wiccans raised in family traditions, I doubt it. For instance, my friend "E.A." tells me he was raised to be a "priest" and that his family's teachings were primarily the knowledge and skills needed to be a priest. (However, a separate, more shamanic set of traditions were also held and transmitted by the family.) Andras Corban Arthen said that his Wiccan family tradition did not include ecstatic or shamanic elements.[8] Another friend, "Lady A" also was brought up as a priestess, not a shaman.

On the other hand, another Witch, "Orion," uses the ancient techniques of drumming and song to enter into a trance or altered state during which she journeys into another world, one with its own geography and residents, in order to bring back information useful to those she considers her community. Andras Corban Arthen leads a group considering itself Wiccan but directed towards developing shamanism within that context.

I and many other Wiccans, however, are not primarily working to develop and control a shamanic altered state. Instead, we teach, we lead people in ritual, we counsel and we inform. While we may work in altered states as a part of our personal spiritual paths, we do not do so to fulfill our obligations to our communities. We probably should not think of ourselves as shamans. Our efforts are more in line with Wicca's ongoing development of a "professional priesthood," clergy who must mesh mundane skills such as keeping accounts, chairing meetings or speaking to the press with counseling, leading worship and developing magical skills.

However, many Wiccan rituals include the "Drawing Down of the Goddess" (or "of the Moon," or "of the God"), and on occasion this approaches the shamanic. The intent is often to literally draw the Goddess into her priestess so that the Goddess may speak through her. While this does not occur during every "drawing down," when it does, few in the circle doubt the non-ordinary quality of the experience. In addition, the dancing, drumming, chanting and guided meditations frequently used in Wiccan circles are similar to traditional shamanic techniques. Because Witches will utilize any technique that will produce the desired effect, a clear classification of of whether or not Wicca is "shamanic" is impossible.

As another example, the "Power Animal Dance"

held for some years at the Pagan Spirit Gathering (see "An Insider's Look at Pagan Festivals" for more on national festivals) certainly uses shamanic techniques. Participants wear costumes portraying their chosen animals, and the ritual is built around ecstatic dancing accompanied by intense drumming. Each person tries to "dance" his or her animal—to move the way the animal moves, to adopt its behavior patterns and in the end to become, in a sense, that animal. The intense identification participants may achieve with their power animals is a step in a shaman's education.

If you want to begin the shamanic journey, there are a number of ways to do so—beyond just the expensive workshops advertised in New Age publications. Historically, ecstatic dancing, guided meditation, drugs of various sorts (but see the caution below), fasting and sensory deprivation have all been successful. The most accessible and usable technique for people who must blend a mundane life with a magical life is shamanic drumming, with the apprentice shaman "riding" the drum's beat toward a vision. It is not necessary to spend a good deal of money and travel elsewhere to follow the shaman's path.

Should you feel drawn to the shamanic path, whether as a Wiccan shaman or otherwise, be prepared for a lot of study, a lot of trance working and a lot of self-searching. The shamanic vision of seeing one's own bones does not necessarily refer only to the physical skeleton!

Wade Grey Fox, publisher of *The Shaman Papers*, states that finding a "power animal" or "guardian spirit" is one of the keys to shamanism. "(T)he power animal is the source of virtually limitless power when worked with properly ... Power animals can be acquired in any of several ways. One, if you are attacked by a wild animal and survive, that may be a sign that the animal that attacked you is your power animal. Two, spontaneous visions. Three, dreams, especially vivid and recurring dreams of a specific animal. Four, during a shamanic journey (and there are specific ways of telling which animals you encounter may be your power animal and which ones are to be avoided)."[9]

Shamanic work begins as you learn to enter into a guided mediation. Tapes and books are available with suitable beginning mediations; some are listed at the end of this chapter. As your meditative abilities develop, you may begin the actual shamanic journey. According to Grey Fox, " . . . it has some aspects of a 'trip' in the 1960s sense of the word, in which your spirit body travels to the Underworld for the purpose of accessing power and/or knowledge, or for healing purposes. The everyday rules of time and space do not apply to the shamanic journey."

Trance is not a deeply mysterious skill available only after years of training. Trance differs among individuals and groups. In essence, it means that you can successfully concentrate your attention on a desired subject, be it a candle flame or the vision of a journey, without serious distraction from the usual world around you.

Once no person who felt an affinity for the shaman's path needed to work alone. Within the clan or tribe were one or more shamans who identified and trained their successors. In our age, we are faced with reinventing those techniques for ourselves. A few teachers are available, in books and in person. Your job is to seek and use these resources while adapting them carefully to your needs and directions. The danger lies in attempting to move too fast. No one can offer you a set two-week (or two-year) training course in shamanism.

Avoid leaping into using drugs, whether legal or not, to speed you on the shaman's path. Mind-altering drugs were and are used in shamanism, but their successful use depended on them being used after extensive and intensive training by an experienced teacher. Casual drug visions have few lasting benefits. Sometimes drug experiences were deliberately employed to approach the near-death experience, and in the hands of any but a real expert the experience might be more than just "near."

The shaman has a special role in a community's spiritual life. He or she can communicate the reality of other worlds as well as entering them on the community's behalf. That our community is not as easily defined as a tribal community does not make it less of one, just less understood. Still, techniques that benefited people in the past are still relevant to people today. Our basic human natures have not changed.

Whether a shaman is "born" or "made" is less important than the fact that becoming a shaman is not easy work. One may be started by a single near-death or visionary experience, but training and development of balance and control are still necessary. The training of the Huichol Indian shaman of Mexico was described by Joan Halifax in *Shamanic Voices* as "extraordinarily complex and demanding, requiring vast knowledge, aesthetic abilities, abundant physical resources and keen social skills."[10] Another tribal shaman quoted in the same book said his apprenticeship spanned a 64-year period.

Indeed, shamanism is the "hard" way out. It begins with the monotonous beat of the drum, the shuffle of dancing feet, the silence of the rock on the the mountaintop, and the disorientation of psychoactive drugs. It does not end.

ABOUT THE AUTHOR

Grey Cat has written articles for many Wiccan and Pagan periodicals, including *Circle Network News*, *Harvest*, and the Covenant of the Goddess newsletter. She is a two-time winner of the Silver Salamander Award for Excellence in Pagan Journalism. She is the co-author with Medicine Hawk of *American Indian Ceremonies*, published by Inner Light Publications. With Michael Ragan she has written a correspondence course called "Herbs for Magick and Medicine." She edited and published *The Crone Papers* for four and a half years, a magazine on the wisdom and magick of the elders.

In the late 1980s she inadvertently founded NorthWind, an American Wicca tradition dedicated to the training of priest/esses and teachers. She sits on the board of directors of Ar n'Draioght Fein, an association of Druids. She has led workshops and rituals at national Pagan gatherings including Pagan Spirit Gathering and Wild Magick and helped organize the Highlands of Tennessee Samhain Gathering in 1990. An enthusiastic convert to computer use, she has compiled a data base on magickal and medicinal use of herbs. Grey Cat lives in the Tennessee hills near the place where she grew up.

NOTES

[1] The word "shaman" comes from a Siberian language. It is both masculine and feminine.

[2] Mircea Eliade, *Shamanism: Archaic Techniques of Ecstasy*. New Yok: Bolingen Foundation, 1951, 1964.

[3] Michael Harner, *The Way of the Shaman*. San Francisco: Harper & Row, 1980.

[4] Otter G'Zell, "Witches and Pagans: In Search of Our Roots" (panel discussion). *Fireheart* 4 (January 1990).

[5] Ibid. Judy Harrow.

[6] Ibid. Isaac Bonewits.

[7] Eliade, *Shamanism*.

[8] Andras Corben Arthen, "Witch as Shaman." *Fireheart* 4 (January 1990).

[9] Wade Grey Fox, *The Shaman Papers*. Vol. 1, No. 1. 907 Iroquois Court, Harrisburg, PA 17109.

[10] Joan Halifax, *Shamanic Voices*. New York: E.P. Dutton, 1979.

SUGGESTIONS FOR FURTHER READING

Bear, Sun. *The Medicine Wheel*. Englewood Cliffs, NJ: Prentice-Hall, 1980.

Drury, Nevil. *Elements of Shamanism*. Shaftesbury (U. K.): Element, 1989.

Eliade, Mircea. *Shamanism: Archaic Techniques of Ecstasy*. New York: Bollingen Foundation, 1951, 1964.

Furst, Peter T. *Hallucinogens and Culture*. Novato, California: Chandler & Sharp, 1976.

Halifax, Joan. *Shamanic Voices*. New York: E. P. Dutton, 1979.

Harner, Michael. *Hallucinogens and Shamanism*. New York: Oxford University Press, 1973, 1981.

_____. *The Way of the Shaman*. San Francisco: Harper & Row, 1980.

Hawk, Medicine and Grey Cat. *American Indian Ceremonies*. New York: Inner Light, 1990.

Jamal, Michele. *Shape Shifters: Shaman Women in Contemporary Society*. London: Arkana 1987.

Kalweit, Holger. *Dreamtime and Inner Space: The World of the Shaman*. Boston: Shambala, 1984.

Nicholson, Shirley, ed. *Shamanism*. Wheaton, Illinois: Theosophical Publishing House, 1987.

Wolfe, Amber. *In the Shadow of the Shaman*. St. Paul: Llewellyn, 1988.

Being a Pagan in a 9-to-5 World

by Valerie Voigt

We all know what Witches are doing on full Moon nights. So what about the other 27 nights ... and all 28 days, for that matter?

While some Witches claim that we are "really no different from anyone else," if we are real Pagans at heart, that is not at all true! Of course, outsiders are disappointed that we don't do all the things they think are so naughty and therefore so exciting. Our spiritual outlook differs from Christianity in several important ways.

To begin with, we are aware of our own goodness and strength, and we are not afraid to admit it. We are not sinners and we know it. We don't have a Devil to blame our mistakes on and we need no Savior to save us from a non-existent Hell. Therefore, we are not guilt-driven. Rather than constantly running from guilt and devils, rather than making futile attempts to "transcend" our own human nature, we embrace our power to choose our actions, and we rejoice in our humanity. Indeed, we work to tune in to our own natures, balancing them with the other forces in the Universe, so that our choices may be worthy of us.

Second, we are one with our Goddess, not separated from Her in the way that most Christians believe they are separated from their God. Our Goddess does not order us around, nor do we grovel before Her. Thus, our religion provides no supportive underpinnings for arbitrary rules, be they imposed on us by other individuals, by groups, or by a government. Useful rules, adaptive rules, however, do find support in our religion—because we see law and custom, properly used, as supporting human life and community. Human life and human community are the basis for most Pagan cultures around the world.

Pagan religions are Nature-centered. Does that mean that to be real Pagans we should all go "back-to-Nature?" Should we leave the cities and live off the land? Hardly: in many areas of the Third World today, the most pressing environmental problems are deforestation from cookfires, and water pollution due to lack of proper sanitation methods. Were we all to return to hunter-gatherer or agricultural village life, the Earth could only support a small fraction of the population it supports now. And do we want to do without penicillin? Without the freedom of communication that we have only because the latest technology allows it?

No, for we know a secret: cities are natural, for we are natural and we created the cities. Computers are natural. Washing machines are natural. Mother Nature is infinite after all! As the Goddess says to one of Her priestesses: "The problem lies not within your toys; the way you use them is what destroys."[1]

I am a "Techno-Pagan" and proud of it, but what does that mean when I walk into my office at 8 a.m.? For one thing, it means that I am doing life-affirming work. Because I do not see this life as one of "doing time until I can die and go to Heaven," I insist, more strongly than most people do, that my work be useful and meaningful and—whenever possible—fun. I avoid doing work for or with companies that pollute the environment or oppress people. I do work that I am proud to do.

This can sometimes be difficult, since the business ethics of America (and most other countries) are basically Satanic. Based both on my personal observations and on statements I have heard and read from corporations and from the politicians they own, these ethics are:

- Make money, and don't worry about whether your methods for doing so are right or wrong.

- If you make a mess or break the law and get caught, try to get out of taking responsibility by blaming someone else.

- Material things are all that really matters. It is more important for the company president to drive a fancy car than for the children of workers at the company's overseas manufacturing plant to have enough to eat.

- Take care of Number One; nobody else matters except to the extent that they are necessary for you to to achieve greater wealth. While there are some businesses whose ethics are more humane, they do not dominate the American or international corporate scene.

Obviously, these ethics are in complete opposition to the life-affirming values of Paganism. Therefore, most Pagans go to extra trouble to find work that is ethically positive. We often end up going into business for ourselves, but the majority of us find positions with businesses that contribute to the greater good of humanity and the Earth. Perhaps this is why so many Pagans end up working for software companies, publishing concerns, and scientific or educational institutions.

We know that choices in life are seldom black-and-white. Some of us do work in businesses that pollute, but when we do, we usually do our part within the company to promote pollution control and beneficial, efficient policies.

Do Pagans find that religion affects their work life in other ways? Yes, sometimes. Some Pagans arrange to have the Sabbat festival days off work. Some are able to make flexible time arrangements to accommodate sleeping late after Full Moon Circles. I know at least one Pagan who works all seven days a week except during her menstrual period, during which she does not work at all. Most Pagans, however, keep the same work schedule as everyone else.

My polytheistic Pagan view is that every situation has many aspects, that there are many different valid ways to view any situation, and that black-and-white viewpoints are not very useful. Therefore, when I go to the office, I do not engage in office politics in the way many people do: when there are conflicting goals or points of view, I recognize that most arguments are not really moral standoffs, but communication blocks. If I can, I get opponents to sit down and talk things over until they can see each other's points of view. Sometimes this leads to a compromise; but if not, the opponents at least let go of their bitterness. Win-win scenarios are often made possible by polytheistic thinking.

I do not hide my religion at work. In some cases, this has made people uncomfortable and in at least one case it got me fired. Most of the time, however, those who are uncomfortable at first relax when they find out what my religion is really about. Sometimes co-workers get very excited about talking to a real Witch, and they want to hear all about it. This means I spend some of my lunch hours involved in educational discussions (after all, I wasn't hired to discuss theology on company time). Sometimes I grow tired of giving what I call my "Pagan PR Spiel," so instead I lend curious co-workers pamphlets, articles, or short books, such as Scott Cunningham's *The Truth About Witchcraft Today*.[2] I remember, though, that part of building a world safe for my Pagan children is telling people the facts about Witchcraft, so I am always willing to answer people's questions.

Paganism's multifaceted, pluralistic small-group culture stands in sharp contrast to the homogenized mass culture of most of the contemporary West. Most Pagans I know are active within a community of fellow Pagans. That community may be a group of a dozen friends who share ceremonies, music, or art, or the worldwide Pagan community with its wide-ranging ritual, arts, literature, music, and newsletters. Pagan newsletters offer the isolated Pagan a small-community-by-mail, and an ever-increasing number of electronic computer bulletin boards (BBS's) do the same (see the last chapter for a partial listing). For many people, Paganism is a full-blown neotribal way of life.

I believe Pagans are in the forefront of an emerging culture in which communities are formed by affinity rather than geography. Still, most of us are also active in local communities. We join park clean-up committees, organize local recycling initiatives, vote in local elections, and usually have clear opinions about local issues.

The typical Pagan small-group orientation often leads Pagans to participate in small-group culture in other ways, as well. Pagans, more than other people, seem to be active in small theater groups, small publishing efforts, small businesses, co-ops, art and discussion groups, and various special-interest and subculture groups and activities such as science fiction fandom, Scottish clan societies, organic gardening associations, and so on. These often have some connection to an aspect of Paganism, such as Nature and environmentalism, ethnic heritage, traditional arts and crafts, or folk dancing and music. I myself am active in so many activities related to Pagan culture that it seldom occurs to me to watch the Great Homogenizer, television.

Pagan Parenting

Pagan parenting is often different from mainstream parenting. Before my daughter Elana was born, my mother-in-law remarked that only in so-called "modern" societies are children separated from their parents all day, and that in the Third World such an arrangement is rare. My husband and I reasoned that only in the past few decades had it become common even in the U.S.A., and that as far as we could see, its impact had been harmful. We looked to Pagan village societies for traditional models. Therefore, we kept Elana strapped onto our chests or backs most of the time when she was tiny, and I stayed home with her for several years. She has always gone almost everywhere with us, has heard (and sometimes contributed to) adult conversations, and has seen many aspects of the world that most other children never see.

Many modern Pagans, the products of nuclear families and high mobility, seek to rediscover the advantages of extended family life. They may live in traditional extended families, or they may live cooperatively with other Pagans, or they may join close-knit covens or traditions which function much like families.

According to research findings, children of such

quasi-extended families in America enjoy most of the
overall advantages of the firstborn children of nuclear
families: higher intelligence, more active imagination,
and so on. These findings are in contrast to the findings
about children raised in Israeli *kibbutzim,* where childcare
is typically a rotating duty like any other task and children may not see their parents very often; children of
kibbutzim may tend to have trouble forming intimate relationships when they become adults.

Pagan parents do not view most childhood behav-
iors as problems. We also tend to avoid lording it over
children, because we are acutely aware that children are
people too and entitled to justice. Some people might
expect this approach to lead to major discipline problems,
but it does not seem to. Children of Pagan parents seldom
get into trouble with the law. They remain closer to their
parents and are less likely to go through teenage rebellion
than other children. Perhaps they have less nonsense to
rebel against.

Pagan parents put relatively little emphasis on obe-
dience and more emphasis on understanding. Pagan kids
can usually expect an explanation for their parents' re-
quests and requirements. Schools may find Pagan parents to be helpful with class enrichment programs, but
uncooperative about convincing maverick children to
conform:

Pagans generally despise conformity for conformity's sake, and many Pagan parents I know have locked
horns with school officials over this issue. Like other mi-
norities, Pagans are beginning to stand their ground and
demand fair treatment of their children.

Like many other Pagan parents, I want to maintain a
unique Pagan cultural identity, and my family participates enthusiastically in our local Pagan community. I
take my daughter Elana to the local sabbats, bardic cir-

cles, and potlucks, where she plays with the other local Pagan kids, and we go to major festivals such as MerryMeet and Pacific Circle when we can.

Our daughter also has three godparents, whose job it is to listen confidentially to her gripes (especially about her parents), to help her face the great questions in life, to pull magical and mundane strings for her if appropriate, and to show her the world. One godparent is a traditional Gardnerian Witch and a school teacher; one is a traditionally-trained but eclectic Witch with Dianic leanings and Jungian interests; and one is a Pagan-sympathetic, forward-looking Quaker who is a musician and computer programmer. When our daughter was born, each brought a blessing to her at her naming ceremony.

Additionally, we are active in the clan-life of the traditions into which our various family members have been initiated, and which have a strong sense of family connection. Since the age of two, Elana has also helped me with paperwork for various Pagan organizations and activities. Thus, while we do not have the benefit of any large Pagan institutions, we certainly have an active quasi-village life!

Certain parenting concerns are of special interest to Pagans. In early motherhood, I felt some concern because I wanted Elana to be able to distinguish between fantasy and reality; yet, as magicians, Witches are constantly dealing with different definitions and concepts of reality, and we use deliberate fantasy as a part of magical training. We speak of altered-consciousness experiences and shamanic phenomena without always bothering to define them as such. Add to this the fact that Elana has been exposed to religious services in a variety of religions; we move in various social, intellectual, and artistic circles, some of which are Pagan and some not; we read Elana books of fairy tales and ancient myths; and we attend science fiction and fantasy conventions, where many people wear costumes and move in and out of different personas with Protean fluidity. Research indicates that even most American *adults* have trouble distinguishing between television and reality. What's a kid to figure is the *real* reality?

In fact, Elana has adjusted beautifully. For one thing, since she first began asking questions about the world, she has phrased them very specifically: "Mom, are there really crocodiles in *this* world?" She seems to know very well which world she means. At the age of five, she is also quite bold about demanding, "Is that for real, or is it just a story?"

Recently, at a science fiction convention, a man walked by in a perfectly crafted Batman costume. Elana pulled my hand: "Mommy, that's Batman! I want to go talk to Batman!"

I thought the costume might be a bit frightening to her if she got that close, so I said, "Gosh, Elana, I'm not sure that's a good idea. I . . ."

"Mom," she interrupted, rolling her eyes and giving me the sort of look usually reserved for parents and idiots, "It's not really Batman. It's only a costume. Give me a break." She let out a sigh, shook her head, and went over to visit Batman.

I am a law-abiding person, but as a Pagan I know that many of the laws of this country were made to favor sectarian Christian views, such as those forbidding free social and sexual expression, whether prohibiting dancing in public or specific sexual acts even between married people. Where possible, conservative Christians have forbidden free religious expression as well: even in the relatively free-wheeling San Francisco Bay area, there are towns which forbid the teaching of Witchcraft as well as banning the use of Tarot cards, magic, and other psychic tools. Until a recent court victory by Witches, New York would only allow two Witches at a time to hold ministerial licenses.

Lawmakers and courts kiss up to the Christian Right all the time. Indeed, recently the Supreme Court revoked legal protection of the right of Native Americans to perform their traditional peyote ritual. If that's not a herald of the New Inquisition, what is?

Some Pagans believe that if we just live quietly, mind our own business, and don't make waves, other people will leave us alone. Having once been a member of the Christian Right (until about 1969), I know better. The religious genocide of the 14th-18th centuries has never really stopped; it has only changed its tactics and become quieter—until recently.

I have been more fortunate than many Pagans in that I personally have suffered little persecution. Other Pagans, however, have had their homes torched or suffered other violence and some have had their children taken away simply because the parents were Pagan. That such outrages occur at all, let alone in the U.S.A., is intolerable. That our own government has cooperated with some of it is even worse, but hardly unexpected. I predict that these problems will grow worse with the Christian conservatives in control of the Supreme Court as well as the rest of the government; many of the conservative Christian groups are growing fervent as the year 2000 (by Christian reckoning) approaches.

On the whole, I believe most Pagans are unaware of the extreme danger from the Christian Right. I also think that if we are to survive, we must organize to protect ourselves by court action and public education. The Jews have set us an excellent example. Pagans, however, generally resist organization: from experience, we tend to suspect that any large organization will be rigid and oppressive. This need not be true of a Pagan-controlled institution, but very large Pagan defense organizations will probably be slow in coming.

In the end most Pagans must come "out of the broom closet" if we are to survive. Staying hidden gives our children the false message that we are ashamed to be Pagans. Not only that, but it gives the same message both to outsiders and to the subconscious of every Pagan. We deserve the right to our identity as much as anyone else on the planet, and we are beginning to claim it.

Meanwhile, I live my life to suit myself and to suit my Goddess, as is my right and my joyful duty.

In the old village cultures, the local Witch was also the local midwife, doctor, and psychologist, as well as magician. Modern Witchcraft has a double inheritance: that of the old village Witches, and that of the old Pagan priesthoods—the Druids, the *Gothis*, and the classical priesthoods of Ishtar, Apollo, and other deities. Should we all be village Witches? Should we be a public priesthood? I have discovered that, however we answer those questions, many people will expect us to do both.

I once worked in a lab where my fellow technicians found out I was a Witch. They found this unusual, but interesting and colorful. One day one of them came over and said, "Valerie, I'm trying to fix this circuit board and nothing seems to work. I've tried everything. This board has to go to the production floor for second shift in an hour. Would you please, um, wiggle your nose or whatever it is you do?"

"Well," I said doubtfully, "I'm really mainly a historian and free spirit rather than a magician. But I can try."

He assured me there would be no hard feelings if the spell did not work. So I concentrated and made some symbolic gestures. He plugged the board in ... and it worked.

"How did you do that?" he shouted. I shrugged. The board went out on schedule and had no further malfunctions.

After that, other co-workers would occasionally bring me their aches and pains and electronic equipment. I treated them all during coffee breaks, mostly with success. Probably the most difficult task was when an employee at another site, an engineer and an adamant atheist, phoned from 600 miles away: his lady friend's cat had been missing for two days, and she was worried sick. Would I try to get it to come home?

"Understand, Val," he added, "I don't believe in any of this weird stuff, but if you can get that cat to come back, I don't care if your methods are weird."

I did what I could. A few hours later, the cat was home. Fortunately, the demand for these Witchy tasks was never heavy enough to interfere with my getting my job done!

Many people, Pagan and otherwise, expect Witches to carry out all the same functions as the full-time paid clergy of the dominant religions. Of course, Witches do magic and perform regular worship ceremonies, as well as rites of occasion and rites of passage (purifications, birthing ceremonies, namings, comings-of-age, marriages, funerals, and the like). Many of us end up doing pastoral counseling, as well. Not all of us are properly prepared to do counseling: most of us have not attended a ministerial school, where pastoral care methods are taught; most of us are not trained in the mental health professions; and most of us have full-time jobs.

This doesn't stop some people from asking us for intensive and time-consuming counseling. Some Witches accept this task, while others do not. The ones which do often burn out at an early age. I believe that if we are going to demand such a full-time commitment from some of our priesthood, we should be prepared to provide them with full-time financial support: after all, isn't their time and energy as valuable as that of the clergy of other religions? Do we value what they do, not just enough to demand that they do it, but enough to reimburse them for their dedicated efforts?

The idea of paying clergy goes against the grain for many Pagans, who think immediately of the rapaciousness of some of the Christian clergy and churches or of some of the New Age teachers. Several older branches of Wicca even altogether forbid the acceptance of money for teaching or practicing the Craft. These prohibitions made excellent sense when Witches were all secretive: each Witch was fully capable of doing everything for herself, and served, at most, a tiny group of people. Nowadays, however, conditions have changed, demands have changed, and needs have changed. As more Pagans form large organizations with complex functions, and as Paganism becomes more public, we will need our leaders to do more than ever. If they are to be able to devote themselves full-time to our needs, we must provide salaries for them.

Another everyday aspect of my religion is that I go out of my way to make, buy, and use products that are gentle to the environment. I don't use spray cans or subscribe to a newspaper. I "precycle" too: that is, I look carefully at a product and at whether I really need it, or whether I can simply do without. Afterward, I recycle everything I can. I even carry my bottles and cans home from work to recycle them. To me, this is simply a tangible form of my worship of Mother Earth.

Summing up, I do not look so different from any of my colleagues in my professional life; I do not even look particularly unusual when I go on TV to be interviewed about the Craft. But what I look like is not what counts;

more important is the way I live my life day-to-day. In the end, that's what really counts in any religion. I am delighted and proud to be a Pagan at the end of the 20th century.

ABOUT THE AUTHOR

Valerie Voigt structured her university curriculum as a Pagan seminary course, earning a degree in classical languages. Since 1980 she has been coordinator-in-chief of the Pagan/Occult/Witchcraft Special Interest Group of Mensa, a nonprofit Pagan networking and educational organization. A practicing Witch since the early 1970s, she makes her living working with computers.

She has trained, worked and taught in several Wiccan traditions, most notably the Gardnerian and Old Faery, and has presented workshops and rituals at major festivals. As an elder in several Wiccan organizations, she is active in national and San Francisco Bay-area Pagan councils, and also lived, studied and worked with Witches of several traditions in Australia. She advises police and community organizations, speaks at colleges, and works for accurate representation of Paganism in the news media.

She has published articles in a variety of Pagan periodicals including *Source, Shadowplay, Isian News, Newsletter of the Centre of the Goddess of Aotearoh, Georgian Monthly, Wiggansnatch, Protean Synthesis, Reclaiming, International Red Garters, Shetotem, Covenant of the Goddess Newsletter, Pagan Parents League Newsletter* and others, as well as writing several books and pamphlets.

Voigt says, "I see myself more than anything else as an opener of doors. I open doors and give people—Pagan and otherwise—opportunities for knowledge, growth, friendship, contact and community. My primary work is among Pagans, but I also do outreach to the larger society because Paganism does not exist in a vacuum. I see any religion that is kept sequestered from the rest of its practitioners' lives as being little more than escapism."

NOTES

[1] Bob Kanefsky, "The Moon Is Also a Satellite." Firebird Arts and Music, 1989.

[2] Scott Cunningham. *The Truth About Witchcraft Today*. St. Paul, Minnesota: Llewellyn Publications, 1988.

Additional Resources

Twenty years ago or more, the would-be Witch was on his or her own in terms of finding teaching or materials. Often people would hear about the Craft and be attracted to it but turn away because it seemed to be inaccessible. Today books, magazines and festivals abound; yet at the same time, the world of the Witches may seem remote. One thing has changed, however: as several contributors to this book have noted, it is now considered legitimate to begin working solo. From the magical viewpoint, solo practice sets up what ceremonial magicians sometimes call an "astral beacon," attracting other people of similar outlook to the practitioner.

In addition, several Craft groups offer beginning instruction by mail, and their advertisements can be found in several of the publications listed below, as well as in others. Being a mail-order student requires a strong degree of self-discipline, but when rightly conducted such a program does offer feedback and advice that might otherwise be unavailable or learned the hard way.

Pagan magazines also carry "personal" ads from groups and covens announcing their general locations, such as "Discussion/study group now meeting in south central New Hampshire ... " These usually screen newcomers by mail before meeting in person. Likewise, individuals place ads seeking fellow souls in their areas. Since many publications have small circulations and are focused on a specific region, such as Southern California or New England, it is best to pick one on the basis of its geographical location before advertising in it.

In any case, the normal common-sense precautions that you would exercise on any blind date or meeting with strangers still hold true. No legitimate Craft group or teacher will request large sums of money, although festivals and special events will have fees that cover renting campgrounds and buildings. Mail-order lessons will require a fee, and only the student can decide if the teaching is worth the price. Furthermore, no legitimate teacher or leader will interfere in a student's personal life to the extent of making job or relationship decisions "for your own progress."

A newcomer to the Craft might also be wary of any leaders who seem to require a constant state of crisis around them. Wicca is a religion of harmony, but there have been some who used the constant threat of "psychic attack," "black magick" and so forth to keep their followers dependent on them.

Witches do not expect their teachers to be rich, drive luxury cars, or live in palaces, but anyone who sets himself or herself up as a teacher or leader should be able to demonstrate that his or her mundane life is under control. While some Pagans do look forward—or backward—to a time of having salaried clergy, at this time virtually no high priestesses or priests are financially supported by their coveners, and those who have expected to be so supported have generally turned out to be frauds. (This does not include income earned through writing, lecturing, astrological readings, or anything else in which a specific service is performed for pay.) More commonly Craft teachers work full-time jobs like anyone else, or else choose part-time employment and the lesser standard of living that goes with it in order to devote themselves to their magical work.

In this simplicity lies some of Witchcraft's strengths. The Craft turns its back on elaborate buildings, complicated holy scriptures and clerical hierarchies in order to offer a "kitchen table" approach to religion. Wiccan priestesses and priests do not often set themselves aside as full-time "holy people," but earn their livings while developing their abilities to shift roles as needed. This, after all, is a potential that can be developed by anyone to some degree. And while money is necessary in everyday life, perhaps the customary Craft approaching of having "lean" organizations with minimal budgets and few large assets has been a healthy thing since it keeps people focused on the essentials.

Because modern Pagans are scattered across all areas of the United States as well as in other nations, small newsletters and medium-sized magazines are essential to the movement. Virtually all Pagan periodicals are published on low budgets by persons and groups who do not make a living from them. While this means they are usually lively and informative, it also means they tend to come and go. Nevertheless, several have lasted over the years, a tribute to the perseverance of their editors.

The list here is not all-inclusive, but represents a short list of the more solid publications as of 1991. Before sending for a subscription, you may wish to write a letter and make sure that the publication is still in existence and that the rates have not changed. As a courtesy to the editor, you should enclose a self-addressed stamped envelope for a reply. A small donation, say $2, would also be a good idea unless a "sample copy price" is specified.

United States

CALENDAR OF EVENTS, c/o Larry Cornett, 9527 Blake Lane #102, Fairfax, Virginia 22031. Pagan festivals and other events of interest.

CIRCLE NETWORK NEWS, P.O. Box 219, Mount Horeb, Wisconsin 53572. Published quarterly. U.S. subscriptions $9 per year bulk mail; $13 first-class mail. Canadian subscriptions U.S. $14. All other countries: U.S. $17 for air mail. Sample issue $3 anywhere. Circle Network News has been published since 1978 and is probably the most widely distributed American Pagan publication. Besides the usual news items, letters, features and short articles, it contains one of the best selections of advertisements and announcements to help Pagans find each other, learn about festivals and so forth.

CONVERGING PATHS, P.O. Box 63, Mount Horeb, Wisconsin 53572. Published quarterly by Branches, "a traditional Wiccan interest group." U.S. and Canadian subscriptions (including membership in Branches), U.S. $13. Foreign air mail $20. Single copies $4 in U.S. or Canada; $6 in other countries. Covers a broad spectrum of Pagan and Wiccan issues.

FIREHEART, P.O. Box 462, Maynard, Massachusetts 01754. Published twice a year by the EarthSpirit Community and described as "a journal of magick and spiritual transformation." Subscriptions are $7 for one year (two issues) in the U.S. and Canada. Single copies $4.

Fireheart is one of the most professionally produced and good-looking of all Pagan magazines and contains lengthy articles, interviews, panel discussions and reviews.

GNOSIS, P.O. Box 14217, San Francisco, California 94114. Published quarterly since 1985. U.S. subscriptions $20 for one year, $40 for two years. Canadian, foreign and library subscriptions U.S. $25 (surface rate). Foreign airmail rate $40. Described as "a journal of the Western inner traditions," this magazine covers a broad spectrum of esoteric thought from occult Judaism to Eastern Orthodoxy to alchemy, hermeticism, and occasional articles on Witchcraft and Paganism. Also available at newsstands.

GREEN EGG, P.O. Box 1542, Ukiah, California 95482. Published quarterly at Samhain, Oimelc, Beltane and Lugnasad. U.S. subscriptions $13 per year, Canadian subscriptions U.S. $18, transatlantic air mail $27, transpacific air mail $30. In its first incarnation, *Green Egg* was the premier Pagan magazine of the late 1960s and early 1970s, published in St. Louis. It was not published for most of the 1980s, but then its founders, now living in California, brought it back to life, and now *Green Egg* is reclaiming its old position as one of the best-edited and most thought-provoking Pagan publications.

HARVEST, P.O. Box 228, S. Framingham, Massachusetts 01701. Published eight times a year. U.S. subscriptions $11, Canadian subscriptions (Can.) $17. All others $25. A Wiccan and Pagan magazine primarily focused on the New England states.

LLEWELLYN PUBLICATIONS, P.O. Box 64383, St. Paul, Minnesota 55164. Write for a free copy of the *Llewel-*

lyn New Times, a combined news magazine on occult and magical topics and mail-order book catalog.

PANEGYRIA, P.O. 57, Index, Washington 98256. Published eight times a year. U.S. subscriptions $12. Published since 1983 by the Aquarian Tabernacle Church (see "Witchcraft and the Law"); primarily focused on the Pacific Northwest region.

RECLAIMING NEWSLETTER, P.O. Box 14404, San Francisco, California 94114. By donation. Ecofeminist Pagan magazine. Lots of thoughtful articles, debates, social and political issues.

Britain

THE CAULDRON. For subscriptions write: M.A. Howard, Caemorgan Cottage, Caemorgan Road, Cardigan, Dyfed, Wales SA 43 1QU, U.K. Published quarterly since 1976. British subscriptions £4. Other European nations, £5 or equivalent cash. U.S. airmail subscriptions $12 (cash only). Australia (Aus) $15 for five issues. A densely packed eclectic Wiccan newsletter with a broad view of the Craft scene in Britain and occasionally elsewhere. Frequent articles on Pagan history and folklore.

QUEST, BCM/SCL Quest, London, WC1N 3XX, England. Another relatively long-lived British magazine devoted to Western magical religion. UK £5 per year. Inquire for foreign subscription rates.

WOOD & WATER, 77 Parliament Hill, London NW3, England. Goddess-oriented ecopagan magazines. £4 per year. Inquire for foreign subscription rates.

Australia

KINDRED SPIRITS QUARTERLY, P.O. Box 101, Bega 2550, New South Wales, Australia. Environmentalist Nature spirituality magazine.

Mail-Order Suppliers

These firms and individuals supply books, ritual items, incense and other materials related to a Wiccan lifestyle. As with the publications, most are small, which means personal service but no guarantee that the company will be there ten years from now. On the other hand, will General Motors be there ten years from now? I have listed only firms with which I am personally acquainted or which have existed long enough to have established a good reputation. Again, you may wish to send a letter with a self-addressed stamped envelope for reply in order to inquire about current catalogs and services.

CAT CREEK HERBS, P.O. Box 227, Florence, Colorado 81226. An extensive catalog of hard-to-find books on shamanism, traditional and folk uses of plants in medicine, daily life and religion, plus books on native plants, herbalism and gardening. Herbal products. Catalog $1.

MARAH, P.O. Box 948, Madison, New Jersey 07940. Hand-blended incenses, perfumes, books and other supplies. Free catalog.

WILDWOOD FRAGRANCES, P.O. Box 403, Boulder, Colorado 80306. Perfumes, potpourris, bath salts, incenses, oils and other items, many named after ancient deities and Pagan festivals and designed for ritual as well as everyday use. They also offer workshops in preparing ritual oils, incenses and beauty products and a mail-order course in Wicca. Catalog $2 (refunded with first order).

General Pagan Organizations

When writing to these organizations, enclose a self-addressed, stamped envelope and enclose a small donation to cover the printing costs of the information you are asking them to send you.

COVENANT OF THE GODDESS, P.O. Box 1226, Berkeley, California 94701. A legal Wiccan church association of covens throughout the English-speaking world. Publishes a newsletter.

FREE SPIRIT ALLIANCE, P. O. Box 5358, Laurel, Maryland 20707. Pagan networking, especially on the East Coast.

PAGAN/OCCULT/WITCHCRAFT SPECIAL INTEREST GROUP, P.O. Box 9336, San Jose, California 95157. A Mensa-affiliated networking, educational, and interest organization. Publishes a newsletter.

Computer Bulletin Boards

Casa de La Luz: (505) 437-8267, 10 p.m. – 6 a.m. daily (New Mexico)

Earth-Rite Forum: (415) 651-9496 (California)

Gemini: (213) 430-8138 (California)

Mysteria: (818) 353-8891 (California)

Philosopher's Stone: (415) 487-9375 (California)

Thelema Net: (415) 751-9308 (California)

Wonderland: (508) 663-6220 (Massachusetts)

Special-Interest Resources

FAMILY TREE, P.O. Box 315, Chestnut Hill, Massachusetts 02167. The focus of this group is on nontraditional extended families.

PAGANS FOR PEACEFUL PARTURITION, P.O. Box 612603, South Lake Tahoe, California 95761, (916) 541-5348. PfPP maintains resource listings and bibliographies available to prospective parents.

CEM Pagan Parent Network, P.O. Box 1652, Bethany, Oklahoma 73008. This is a nationwide organization.

SOUTHWEST GAY AND LESBIAN PAGAN COALITION, P.O. Box 26442, Oklahoma City, Oklahoma. This organization is growing into a nationwide network.

GREAT MOTHER'S LOVE, P.O. Box 42, Fairfield, Vermont 05455. These people run a pen-pal network for Pagan kids and hold an annual festival for Pagan families.

PAGAN PARENTING NETWORK, c/o Nicola Beechsquirrel, Blaenberen, Mynyddcerrig, Llanelli, Dyfed, Cymru (Wales) SA 15 5BL, U.K. PPN includes many members around the British Isles and elsewhere.

PAGAN PARENTS' ASSOCIATION, P.O. Box 2643, Seattle, Washington 98111. Members are in many states, but especially the Seattle area.

CHILDREN OF THE EARTH, P.O. Box 166, Berkeley Springs, West Virginia 25541-0116. This newsletter is by and for Pagan families with children.

HAM (How About Magic?), P.O. Box 1542, Ukiah, California 95482, (707) 485-7787. This is a magazine for Pagan kids aged 8 to 15. Subscriptions $6/year.

THE LITTLEST UNICORN, P.O. Box 8814, Minneapolis, Minnesota 55408. This newsletter for Pagan children has been publishing for several years.

PAGAN SPIRIT GATHERING, c/o P.O. Box 219, Mt. Horeb, Wisconsin 53572, (608) 924-2216 This annual summer festival includes activities for Pagan children and teens.

Stay in Touch. . .

**Llewellyn publishes hundreds of books
on your favorite subjects**

On the following pages you will find listed some books now available on related subjects. Your local bookstore stocks most of these and will stock new Llewellyn titles as they become available. We urge your patronage.

Order by Phone

Call toll-free within the U.S. and Canada, **1–800–THE MOON**.
In Minnesota call **(612) 291–1970**.
We accept Visa, MasterCard, and American Express.

Order by Mail

Send the full price of your order (MN residents add 7% sales tax) in U.S. funds to:

**Llewellyn Worldwide
P.O. Box 64383, Dept. L377-9
St. Paul, MN 55164–0383, U.S.A.**

Postage and Handling

◆ $4.00 for orders $15.00 and under
◆ $5.00 for orders over $15.00
◆ No charge for orders over $100.00

We ship UPS in the continental United States. We cannot ship to P.O. boxes. Orders shipped to Alaska, Hawaii, Canada, Mexico, and Puerto Rico will be sent first-class mail.
International orders: Airmail—add freight equal to price of each book to the total price of order, plus $5.00 for each non-book item (audiotapes, etc.). Surface mail—Add $1.00 per item.
Allow 4–6 weeks delivery on all orders. Postage and handling rates subject to change.

Group Discounts

We offer a 20% quantity discount to group leaders or agents. You must order a minimum of 5 copies of the same book to get our special quantity price.

Free Catalog

Get a free copy of our color catalog, *New Worlds of Mind and Spirit*. Subscribe for just $10.00 in the United States and Canada ($20.00 overseas, first class mail). Many bookstores carry *New Worlds*—ask for it!

WITCHCRAFT TODAY, BOOK II, Rites of Passage
edited by Chas S. Clifton

The ritual glue that binds Pagan culture and a wide view and a living Pagan culture are presented in this book. *Witchcraft Today, Book Two: Rites of Passage,* therefore, is organized by birth, puberty, adulthood, partnership, parenthood, Wicca conversion, maturity or eldership, and finally death.

- Childbirth and Wiccaning—Patricia Telesco
- Raising a Pagan Child—Karen Charboneau-Harrison
- Late Adolescence and Early Adulthood—Anodea Judith
- Working with the Underaged Seeker—Judy Harrow
- Reflections on Conversion to Wicca—by Darcie
- Initiation by Ordeal: Military to Adulthood—by Judy Harrow
- Modern Pagan Marriage— by Jeff Charboneau-Harrison
- Puberty Rites for Adult Women—by Oz
- Pagan Illness Approaches, Grief and Loss— by Paul Suliin
- Witches after 40—by Grey Cat
- Pagan Rites of Dying—by Oz

0-87542-378-7, 288 pgs., 5 ¼ x 8, softcover   **$9.95**

WITCHCRAFT TODAY, BOOK III, Witchcraft & Shamanism
edited by Chas S. Clifton

This book is a compelling and honest examination of shamanic techniques as presently practiced in Neopagan Witchcraft. Shamanism is a natural adjunct to the ritualistic and magical practice of many covens and solitary Pagans. How others have integrated techniques such as trance journeys, soul retrieval, and altered states of consciousness is discussed.

Discover how shamanic ideas influenced Greek philosophers, Platonists, Pythagoreans and Gnostics ... learn how evidence from the old witch trials suggests that Europeans may have practiced shamanic journeying ... incorporate caves for ritual and inner journeys ... find out who is out there retrieving souls and curing elfshot ... compare the guided visualizations common to modern magickal practice with the neo-shamanic journey ... learn how spirit contacts are made ... and more.

1-56718-150-3, 288 pgs., 5 ¼ x 8, photos, softbound   **$9.95**